FALK
LINLITHGOW

www.philips-maps.co.uk

First published 2008 by

Philip's, a division of
Octopus Publishing Group Ltd
www.octopusbooks.co.uk
2–4 Heron Quays
London E14 4JP
An Hachette Livre UK Company
www.hachettelivre.co.uk

First edition 2008
First impression 2008

ISBN 978-0-540-09366-3

To the best of the Publishers' knowledge, the information in this atlas was correct at the time of going to press. No responsibility can be accepted for any errors or their consequences.

The representation in this atlas of a road, track or path is no evidence of the existence of a right of way.

Printed and bound in China by Toppan

Contents

II **Key to map symbols**

III **Key to map pages**

IV **Route planning**

2 **Street maps** at 4½ inches to 1 mile

58 **Index**

68 **List of numbered locations**

Key to map symbols

Roads

Motorway with junction number

Primary route – dual/single carriageway

A road – dual/single carriageway

B road – dual/single carriageway

Through-route – dual/single carriageway

Minor road – dual/single carriageway

Rural track, private road or narrow road in urban area

Path, bridleway, byway open to all traffic, road used as a public path

Road under construction

Pedestrianised area

Gate or obstruction to traffic restrictions may not apply at all times or to all vehicles

Parking, Park and Ride

Railways

Railway

Miniature railway

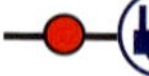

Metro station, private railway station

Emergency services

Ambulance station, coastguard station

Fire station, police station

Hospital, Accident and Emergency entrance to hospital

General features

Place of worship, Post Office

Information centre (open all year)

Bus, coach station

Important buildings, schools, colleges, universities and hospitals

Woods, built-up area

Tumulus FORT Non-Roman antiquity, Roman antiquity

Leisure facilities

Camping site, caravan site

Golf course, picnic site

Boundaries

Postcode boundaries

County and unitary authority boundaries

Water features

River Ouse

Tidal water, water name

Non-tidal water – lake, river, canal or stream

Lock, weir

Scales

Blue pages: 4½ inches to 1 mile 1:14 080

0 220 yds ¼ mile 660 yds ½ mile

0 125m 250m 375m ½ km

Adjoining page indicators The colour of the arrow and the band indicates the scale of the adjoining page (see above)

Abbreviations

Abbreviation	Meaning	Abbreviation	Meaning
Acad	Academy	Mkt	Market
Allot Gdns	Allotments	Meml	Memorial
Cemy	Cemetery	Mon	Monument
C Ctr	Civic Centre	Mus	Museum
CH	Club House	Obsy	Observatory
Coll	College	Pal	Royal Palace
Crem	Crematorium	PH	Public House
Ent	Enterprise	Recn Gd	Recreation Ground
Ex H	Exhibition Hall	Resr	Reservoir
Ind Est	Industrial Estate	Ret Pk	Retail Park
IRB Sta	Inshore Rescue Boat Station	Sch	School
		Sh Ctr	Shopping Centre
Inst	Institute	TH	Town Hall/House
Ct	Law Court	Trad Est	Trading Estate
L Ctr	Leisure Centre	Univ	University
LC	Level Crossing	Wks	Works
Liby	Library	YH	Youth Hostel

Key to map pages

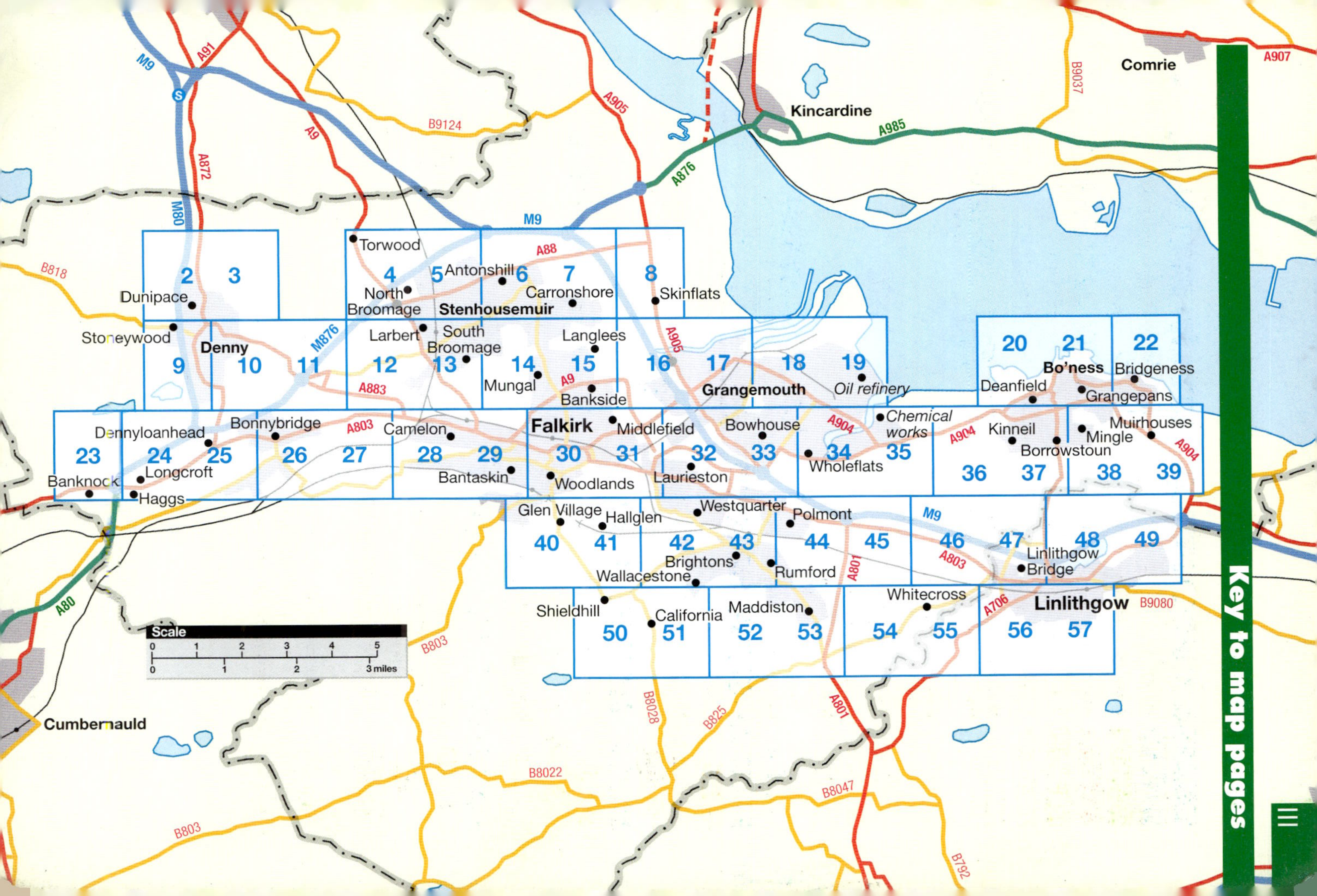

Route planning
Scale
0 1 2 3 4 km
Coxet Hill
Broombridge
Borestone
St.Ninians
BANNOCKBURN HERITAGE CENTRE
Whins of Milton
Bannockburn
Fallin
Throsk
KERSIE RD.
Mains of Throsk
South Alloa
Kersie Mains
Burnhead
Chartershall
M9
A872
A9
A91
A905
B9124
Hilton
Cowie
Dunmore Moss
Dunmore
RIVER
Sauchieburn Ho.
Foot o' Green
North Third Res.
Stirling Services
Gartclush
Dunmore Park
THE PINEAPPLE
Cauldbarns
Old Sauchie
Auchenbowie
Sauchenford
Hillhead
Whitehill
Westfield
Milnholm
Craigend
M80
W. Plean
Plean
PLEAN
Barr Wood
Avenuehead
Bridge-end
Airth Mains
Myres
Muirmailing
Plean Ho.
Airth Castle
Coulter Res
Hall Quarter
Carbrook Mains
Letham Moss
Letham
Northfield
Drum of Kinneard
Willsfield
Torwood
Carron
Quarter Ho.
STIRLING
BELLSDYKE
B818
Langhill
Tor Wood
A88
Bensfield
Burnhouse
Carron Glen
Tod Hill
Antonshill
Overton
Dunipace
Doghillock
North Broomage
OCHILVIEW
Stenhousemuir
B905
Fankerton
Stoneywood
Denny
M876
Larbert
LARBERT
Carronshore
Carron
Langlees
Myot Hill
Garth
A883
Housefill
South Broomage
Castlerankie
A872
B905
B902
Bainsford
Leys
Cuthelton
Roman Camp (site of)
Glenhead
Drumbowie
Little Denny Res.
Head of Muir
Bogton
Bankside
B906
Drumbowie Res.
Roman Fort (site of)
Bankhead
Bonny Water
A803
Middle
FIRS PARK
CAMELON
Banknock
FALKIRK RD.
Wester Carmuirs
Braeface
P&R
Forth and Clyde Canal
Camelon
Grahamston
GRAHAMSTON
A904
ANTONINE WALL
Cowden Hill
M80
Dennyloanhead
Bonnybridge
ROUGH CASTLE
FALKIRK WHEEL
Cloybank RD.
Parkfoot
Tamfourhill
Bantaskin
KILSYTH
Longcroft
Milnquarter
B816
CALLENDAR HOUSE
Banknock
Haggs
Greenhill
High Bonnybridge
Howierig
1746
HIGH
FALKIRK
Callendar
Auchinloch
A80
Woodend
Greenrig
B803
Hall
South Woodend
Forresterquarter
Drum Wood
Glen Village
Roman Fort (site of)
Castlecary
Craigieburn
Glenrig
B8028
Castle Cary
Blackhill
South Drum
Wardpark
Walton
Castlecary High Wood
Tippetcraig
Auchengean
Shieldhall
Rottenstocks
FALKIRK
Walton Burn
Barleyside
Abronhill
Arns
Garbethill Ho.
Wester Jawcraig
Easter Jawcraig
High Stanerig
Gardrum Moss
Kildrum
Glenhead
Garbethill Muir
Jawcraig
L. Ellrig
CUMBERNAULD
Fannyside Muir
Nappiefaulds Ho.
Threaprig
Easter Fannyside
B803
Oakerdykes
Lenziemill
B8054
Fannyside Lochs
Dyke
Easter Loanrigg
Boxton
Grangeneuk
River Avon
Slamannan
Crossburn
Palacerigg
Waterhead
PALACERIGG
B8022
Neucks
Luggiebank
Balcastle Ho.
Glenhove
Wester Glentore
Binniehill
Babbithill
Coathill
Muirhead
B8022
B825
Boglea
Easter Glentore
Lodge Fm.
Easter Drumclair
Langdales

V
Kincardine Bridge
Kincardine
Devilla Forest
FORTH
A985
A876
A907
A977
B9037
Kennet
Kilbagie
Kennetpans
Airth
Blairhall
Comrie
Oakley
High Valleyfield
Low Valleyfield
Culross
CULROSS PALACE
Abbey
Torryburn
Newmills
Low Torry
Torry Bay
Preston Island
Longannet Pt.
Crombie Pt.
Mains of Powfoulis
Stonehouse
Howkerse
Skinflats
Docks
River Carron
GRANGEMOUTH
Oil Refinery
Glensburgh
FALKIRK STADIUM
M9
A905
A904
B9132
B9143
Wholeflats
Bo'ness
BO'NESS & KINNEIL RLY.
KINNEIL HO.
Grangepans
Carriden
Bridgeness
Newton
Maidenpark
Kinneil
Borrowstoun Mains
Muirhouses
A993
A706
A904
B903
Walton
Grougfoot
Laurieston
Beancross
Westquarter
WESTQUARTER DOVECOTE
Redding
Polmont
POLMONT
Polmont Station
Brightons
Rumford
Lathallan
Inveravon
Polmonthill
Upr. Kinneil
BIRKHILL
CLAY MINE
Muirhouse
Gardners Hall
A803
B8029
Linlithgow Bridge
Linlithgow
PALACE
B9080
Kingsfield
Kingscavil
Wallacestone
Redding Muir
Maddiston
Whitecross
Works
A801
B825
Manuel Ho.
1526
Blackbraes
Craigend
Whiterigg
Loan
MUIRAVONSIDE
Muiravonside Ho.
Castle
Blackrig
Greyrigg
Standburn
Candie
Candie-ond
R. Avon
Blackston
Blackfaulds
Westfield
B8028
B8047
B8810
A706
W. Woodside
Lochcote Res
TORPHICHEN PRECEPTORY
Torphichen
Cairnpapple Hill
Williamcraigs
Preston Ho.
Cockleroy 278
BEECRAIGS WOOD
Beecraigs Wood
Whitebaulks
Riccarton Hills
Nth. Mains
Blackcraig
Parkley Pl.
Cauldhame
Riccarton
W. Ochiltree
Bridgend
Muirhead
Kirkton
Shires Mill
Over Inzievar
Inzievar Wood
Langleas
Duck Hill
Drumfin
Torrie Ho.
Cowstrandburn
Sunnyside
Shepherdlands
Lochshaw Moss
Bath Moor Plantn.
Haldane Ho.
Bogside
Burrowine
Bluther Burn
Righead
Peppermill Dam
Tulliallan Castle
Moor L.
Culross Moor
Bordie
Inch Fm.
Blair Castle
Dunimarle Castle
Blairburn
Kincardine on Forth Bridge
Broadcarse
Loanside
Castle
Arns
Kennet Ho
Alane
Blair Ho.
Newbigging
Comrie Burn
E. Kerse Mains
Carriden Ho.
Kinglass
Stacks
Cauldcoats Holdings
Res.
Park
Glensburgh
A9
Wallacestone
Greyrigg

Northfield Quarry
M80 Stirling
A872 Stirling
Wellsfield Farm
Braes Wood
High Quarter Farm
Quarter Wood
Braes
Old Quarter
Burnhouse
Low Quarter Mill
Croftfoot
Broomhill Farm
M80
FK6
Roseban
Avon Burn
A872
STIRLING ST
Banken
Dunipace
Dunipace Prim Sch
Drumelzier
Herbertshire Castle Park
Risk
Denny Bridge
River Carron
Mill
Stoneywood
B818
TARDUFF PL
STONEYWOOD PK
A883
Denny Prim Sch
KNIGHTS WAY
ST JOHN'S
DUKE ST
WILSON AVE
ROSEMARY CT
CASTLE TERR
BRIDGE CRES
WALLACE CRES
GROVE ST
HUNTER GDNS
BREWSTER PL
WEST BORELAND RD
BARNEGO RD
HAZEL CRES
HAWTHORN DR
CHESTNUT CRES
BEECH CRES
LINDEN AVE
LAIROX TERR
PO
CHURCH LA
MILTON PL
CRATHIE DR
BRAEMAR GDNS
KILBIRNIE TER
AVON ST
NORTHFIELD RD
JOHN DAVIDSON DR
MEADOW CT
CONNOLLY DR
MAPLE PL
TYGETSHAUGH CT
THISTLE AVE
LAUREL CT
AVONBANK GDNS
AVONSIDE DR
LOUDENS WLK
INGLESTON AVE
BROOMHILL PL
CROFTFOOT PL
RULLEY VIEW
KIRKLAND DR
HOOKNEY TERR
A
B
C
85
84
83
80
9
4
3
2
1

A
B
C
Langlands
Dales Wood
Quarter House
85
4
3
FK6
84
Doghillock
Pamphellgoat Wood
2
Toptowie Hill
DENOVAN RD
MILTON ROW
Denovan Mains
Denovan
1
VALE PL
QUEENS DR
CARRONSIDE PL
DUNBAR GATE
St Patrick's RC Prim Sch
WINCHESTER AVE
Winchester Avenue Ind Est
River Carron
83
KELLY DR
McTAGGART AVE
GILL PK
CHURCH WLK
Liby
STIRLING ST
DAVIES ROW
HERBERTSHIRE ST
HERBERTSHIRE ST
KIRKSLAP
SPRINGFIELD RD
Sewage Works
Kirkland
111
82
WINCHESTER DR
BROAD ST
BROAD ST
GLEBE ST
PO

A9 Stirling
A
B
C
GLEN RD
CASTLE CRES
NEWINGTON LA
FORRESTER GAIT
85
Torwood
Whinnie Muir
4
Torwood Sch
Glenbervie House
3
Torwoodhead
A9 STIRLING RD
FK5
CH
84
M876
Tod Hill
2
GLENBERVIE
North Broomage
STIRLING RD
A9
BELLSDYKE RDBT
2
A88
M876
Baxter Wood
TAPPOCH PL
OLD BELLSDYKE RD
NORTH BROOMAGE RDBT
1
LOGIE DR
OLD DENNY RD
The Royal Scottish National
GLENBERVIE
Oakbank Wood
83
H
LADYWELL CT
M876
Big Wood
84
A
12
B
85
C

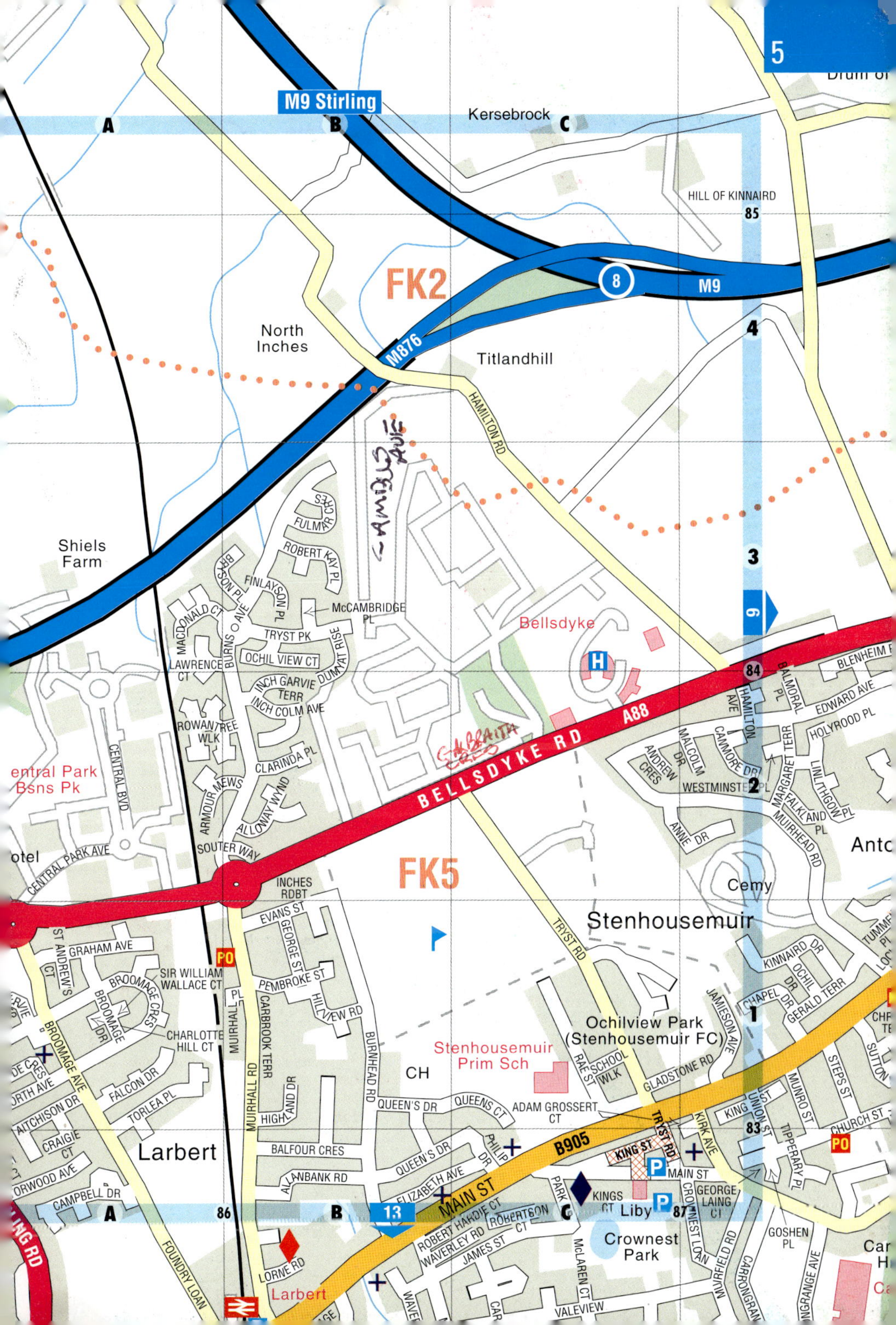
M9 Stirling
A
B
C
Kersebrock
HILL OF KINNAIRD
85
FK2
8
M9
M876
North Inches
Titlandhill
4
HAMILTON RD
Shiels Farm
3
9
FULMAR CRES
ROBERT KAY PL
BRYSON PL
FINLAYSON PL
McCAMBRIDGE PL
MACDONALD CT
BURNS AVE
TRYST PK
DUMYAT RISE
OCHIL VIEW CT
LAWRENCE CT
INCH GARVIE TERR
INCH COLM AVE
Bellsdyke
84
BLENHEIM PL
BALMORAL PL
EDWARD AVE
HOLYROOD PL
HAMILTON AVE
A88
BELLSDYKE RD
ROWANTREE WLK
CLARINDA PL
ANDREW CRES
MALCOLM DR
CANMORE DR
MARGARET TERR
LINLITHGOW PL
Central Park Bsns Pk
CENTRAL BVD
ARMOUR MEWS
ALLOWAY WYND
WESTMINSTER PL
2
FALKLAND PL
ANNE DR
MUIRHEAD RD
SOUTER WAY
CENTRAL PARK AVE
INCHES RDBT
FK5
Cemy
Stenhousemuir
EVANS ST
GEORGE ST
ST ANDREW'S CT
GRAHAM AVE
PO
SIR WILLIAM WALLACE CT
PEMBROKE ST
TRYST RD
KINNAIRD DR
OCHIL DR
BROOMAGE CRES
BROOMAGE DR
MUIRHALL PL
CARBROOK TERR
HILLVIEW RD
JAMIESON AVE
CHAPEL DR
GERALD TERR
1
CHARLOTTE HILL CT
Ochilview Park (Stenhousemuir FC)
BROOMAGE AVE
MUIRHALL RD
BURNHEAD RD
Stenhousemuir Prim Sch
FALCON DR
CH
RAE ST
SCHOOL WLK
GLADSTONE RD
STEPS ST
MUNRO ST
SUTTON
TORLEA PL
HIGHLAND DR
QUEEN'S DR
QUEENS CT
ADAM GROSSERT CT
AITCHISON DR
TRYST RD
KING ST
UNION ST
83
CHURCH ST
CRAIGIE CT
Larbert
BALFOUR CRES
PHILIP DR
B905
KING ST
KIRK AVE
TIPPERARY PL
PO
QUEEN'S DR
P
MAIN ST
ALLANBANK RD
ELIZABETH AVE
PARK
KINGS CT
GEORGE LAING CT
CAMPBELL DR
MAIN ST
86
13
Liby
87
A
B
C
ROBERT HARDIE CT
ROBERTSON CT
CROWNEST LOAN
MUIRFIELD RD
GOSHEN PL
WAVERLEY RD
JAMES ST
Crownest Park
CARRONGRANGE AVE
FOUNDRY LOAN
LORNE RD
McLAREN CT
Larbert
VALEVIEW

Drum of Kinnaird
HILL OF KINNAIRD
M876
M9
FK2
Kinnaird House
HAMILTON RD
ANTONSHILL RDBT
A88
BELLSDYKE RD
Bellsdyke
B902
CARRON RD
B905
Antonshill
FK5
Cemy
Stenhousemuir
KING ST
TRYST RD
Ochilview Park (Stenhousemuir FC)
Stenhousemuir Prim Sch
NEW CARRON RD
Carron Prim Sch
STENHOUSE RD
CARRON RDBT
Carron
Crownest Park
Liby
Carron Hill
Carrongrange Sch
1 BARRA PL
2 ROXBURGH PL
3 NEIDPATH DR
4 CRATHES AVE

7
M876 Kincardine Bridge
(A876)
Southfield
A
B
C
85
M9
7
M876
4
Muirdyke Burn
A88
BELLSDYKE RD
3
8
FK2
Bensfield
84
Kirkton
2
Carronshore Prim Sch
CARRONHALL AVE
KINNAIRD AVE
QUARROLHALL CRES
GAIRDOCH DR
SYMINGTON PL
BRUCE CRES
WEBSTER AVE
KINCARDINE RD
LONGDYKE PL
MOFFAT AVE
CUTTYFIELD PL
SKAITHMUIR CRES
SKAITHMUIR AVE
ROUGHLANDS CRES
Carronshore
AUCHENTYRE PL
Westertown
LADYSGATE CT
FERN LEA GR
KIRKTON PL
MUIRDYKE AVE
NORTH MAIN ST
WESTERTON TERR
BOTHKENNAR RD
1
CHAPEL CRES
BLACKMILL CRES
BURNSIDE PL
BURNSIDE PL
MILL RD
MILL CT
DUNCAN AVE
RAE CT
MAIN ST
PO
FRIENDSHIP GDNS
CASTLE AVE
CARRONSHORE RD
WATERS END
THE MEADOWS
LORIMAR PL
MONTGOMERY DR
BRYCE AVE
THE AVENUE
Carron House
83
HALKET CRES
DOCK ST
89
B
16
C
90
A
River Carron
CAMERON PL
CHAMBERS DR
MYLNE PL
BRYCE AVE
ANDERSON DR
GILFILLAN PL
WARDLAW PL
CARRONBANK CT
M9
Back Fa
Sou Bellsc
ands

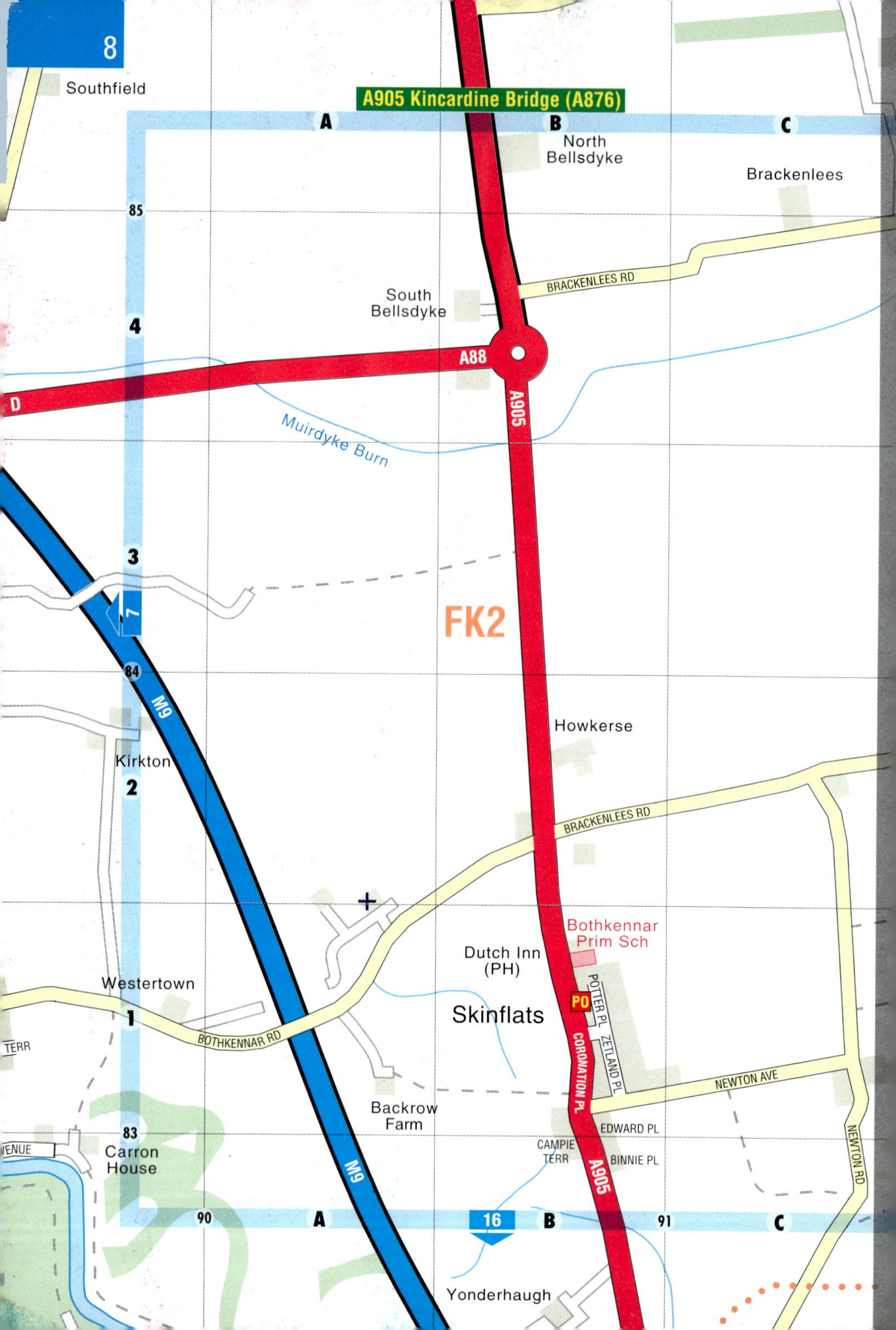
8
Southfield
A905 Kincardine Bridge (A876)
A
B
C
North Bellsdyke
Brackenlees
85
BRACKENLEES RD
South Bellsdyke
4
A88
D
A905
Muirdyke Burn
3
7
FK2
84
M9
Howkerse
Kirkton
2
BRACKENLEES RD
Bothkennar Prim Sch
Dutch Inn (PH)
Westertown
PO
POTTER PL
Skinflats
1
BOTHKENNAR RD
CORONATION PL
ZETLAND PL
TERR
NEWTON AVE
Backrow Farm
EDWARD PL
83
CAMPIE TERR
BINNIE PL
NEWTON RD
ENUE
Carron House
A905
M9
90
A
16
B
91
C
Yonderhaugh

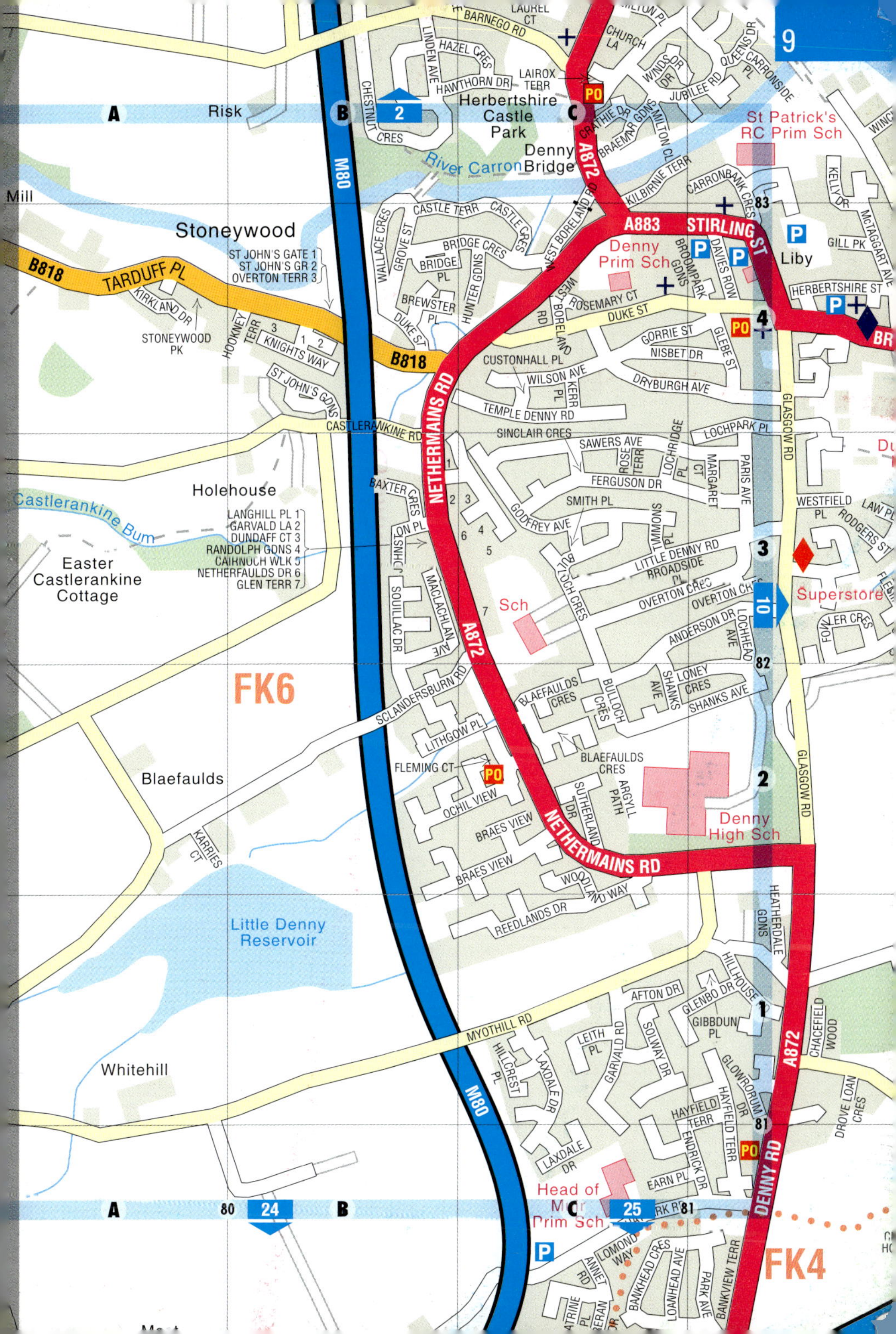

A
B
C
2
Risk
Herbertshire
Castle
Park
Denny
Bridge
River Carron
Mill
Stoneywood
B818
TARDUFF PL
KIRKLAND DR
STONEYWOOD PK
HOOKNEY TERR
KNIGHTS WAY
ST JOHN'S GDNS
ST JOHN'S GATE 1
ST JOHN'S GR 2
OVERTON TERR 3
M80
BARNEGO RD
LAUREL CT
HAZEL CRES
LINDEN AVE
HAWTHORN DR
CHESTNUT CRES
LAIROX TERR
CHURCH LA
MILTON PL
WINDSOR DR
JUBILEE RD
QUEENS DR
CARRONSIDE
CRATHIE DR
BRAEMAR GDNS
MILTON CL
A872
PO
St Patrick's RC Prim Sch
KILBIRNIE TERR
CARRONBANK CRES
KELLY DR
McTAGGART AVE
GILL PK
83
A883
STIRLING ST
Liby
HERBERTSHIRE ST
BR
Denny Prim Sch
BROOMPARK GDNS
DAVIES ROW
ROSEMARY CT
DUKE ST
WEST BORELAND RD
CASTLE TERR
CASTLE CRES
WALLACE CRES
GROVE ST
BRIDGE CRES
BRIDGE PL
HUNTER GDNS
BREWSTER PL
DUKE ST
4
GORRIE ST
NISBET DR
GLEBE ST
CUSTONHALL PL
WILSON AVE
KERR PL
DRYBURGH AVE
TEMPLE DENNY RD
NETHERMAINS RD
CASTLERANKINE RD
SINCLAIR CRES
SAWERS AVE
ROSE TERR
LOCHRIDGE PL
MARGARET CT
PARIS AVE
LOCHPARK PL
GLASGOW RD
FERGUSON DR
SMITH PL
TIMMONS PL
GODFREY AVE
WESTFIELD PL
LAW PL
RODGERS ST
Du
Holehouse
Castlerankine Burn
LANGHILL PL 1
GARVALD LA 2
DUNDAFF CT 3
RANDOLPH GDNS 4
CAIRNOCH WLK 5
NETHERFAULDS DR 6
GLEN TERR 7
Easter Castlerankine Cottage
BAXTER CRES
JOHNSTON PL
SOUILLAC DR
MACLACHLAN AVE
LITTLE DENNY RD
BROADSIDE PL
BULLOCH CRES
OVERTON CRES
3
10
Superstore
Sch
ANDERSON DR
LOCHHEAD AVE
FOWLER CRES
FK6
82
SCLANDERSBURN RD
BLAEFAULDS CRES
BULLOCH CRES
SHANKS AVE
LONEY CRES
LITHGOW PL
FLEMING CT
BLAEFAULDS CRES
OCHIL VIEW
Blaefaulds
SUTHERLAND DR
ARGYLL PATH
2
Denny High Sch
BRAES VIEW
KARRIES CT
WOODLAND WAY
REEDLANDS DR
HEATHERDALE GDNS
Little Denny Reservoir
HILLHOUSE
AFTON DR
GLENBO DR
GIBBDUN PL
1
MYOTHILL RD
HILLCREST PL
LAXDALE DR
LEITH PL
GARVALD RD
SOLWAY DR
GLOWRORUM DR
CHACEFIELD WOOD
Whitehill
HAYFIELD TERR
ENDRICK DR
81
DROVE LOAN CRES
EARN PL
DENNY RD
Head of Muir Prim Sch
80
24
25
81
LOMOND WAY
ANNET RD
BANKHEAD CRES
LOANHEAD AVE
PARK AVE
BANKVIEW TERR
FK4
P

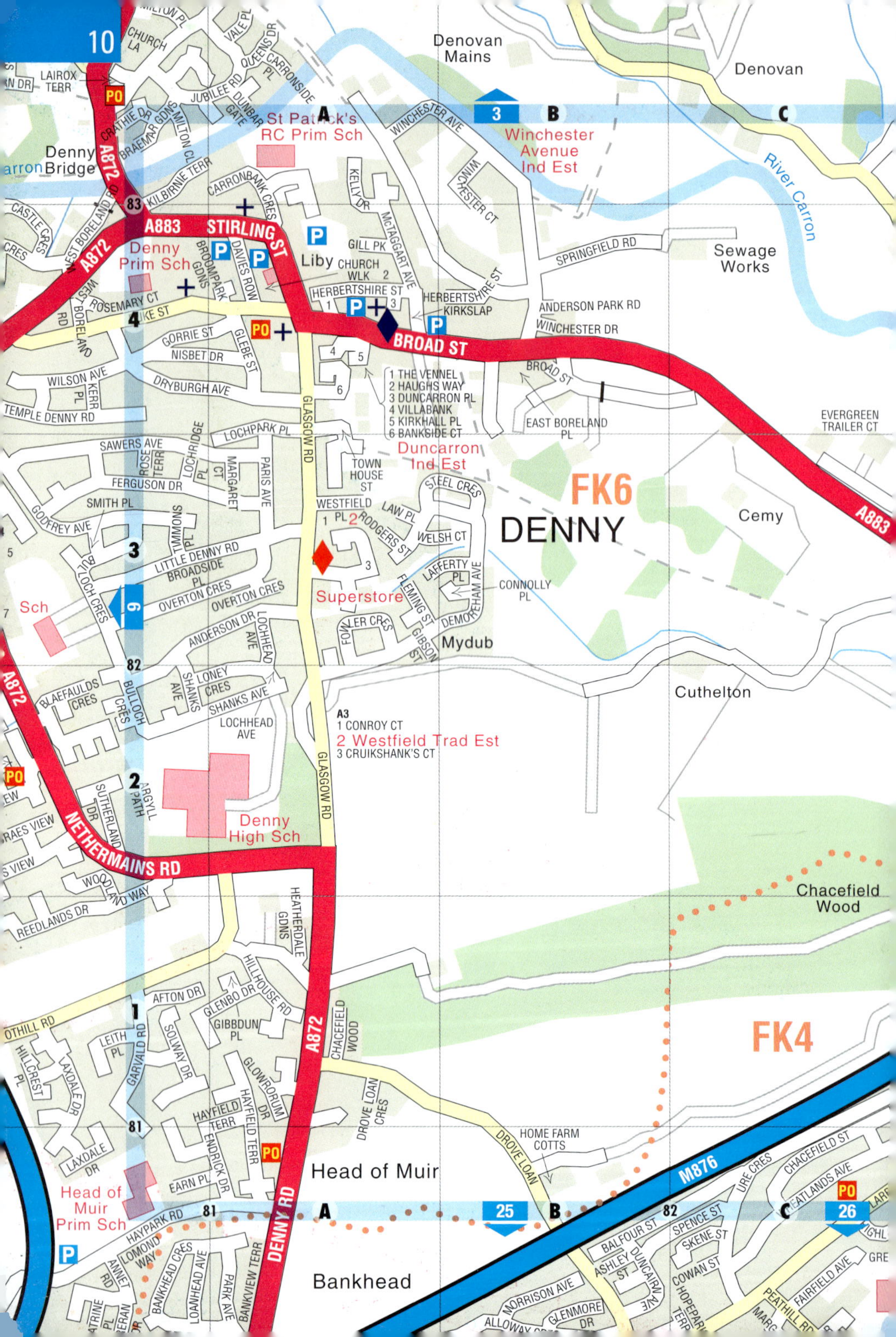
10
Denovan Mains
Denovan
3
A
B
C
St Patrick's RC Prim Sch
Winchester Avenue Ind Est
River Carron
Denny Bridge
A872
A883
83
STIRLING ST
Denny Prim Sch
Liby
Sewage Works
BROAD ST
4
LAIROX TERR
CHURCH LA
MILTON PL
VALE PL
QUEENS DR
CARRONSIDE
JUBILEE RD
DUNBAR GATE
CRATHIE DR
BRAEMAR GDNS
MILTON CL
KILBIRNIE TERR
CARRONBANK CRES
WINCHESTER AVE
WINCHESTER CT
KELLY DR
MCTAGGART AVE
GILL PK
CHURCH WLK
HERBERTSHIRE ST
KIRKSLAP
SPRINGFIELD RD
ANDERSON PARK RD
WINCHESTER DR
CASTLE CRES
WEST BORELAND RD
BROOMPARK GDNS
DAVIES ROW
ROSEMARY CT
DUKE ST
GORRIE ST
NISBET DR
GLEBE ST
WILSON AVE
KERR PL
DRYBURGH AVE
TEMPLE DENNY RD
1 THE VENNEL
2 HAUGHS WAY
3 DUNCARRON PL
4 VILLABANK
5 KIRKHALL PL
6 BANKSIDE CT
EAST BORELAND PL
EVERGREEN TRAILER CT
Duncarron Ind Est
LOCHPARK PL
SAWERS AVE
ROSE TERR
LOCHRIDGE PL
MARGARET CT
PARIS AVE
GLASGOW RD
TOWN HOUSE ST
FERGUSON DR
SMITH PL
GODFREY AVE
TIMMONS PL
STEEL CRES
WESTFIELD PL
LAW PL
RODGERS ST
WELSH CT
FK6
DENNY
Cemy
3
LITTLE DENNY RD
BROADSIDE PL
OVERTON CRES
BULLOCH CRES
LAFFERTY PL
CONNOLLY PL
FLEMING ST
DEMOREHAM AVE
Superstore
Sch
9
ANDERSON DR
LOCHHEAD AVE
FOWLER CRES
GIBSON ST
Mydub
82
BLAEFAULDS CRES
LONEY CRES
SHANKS AVE
Cuthelton
LOCHHEAD AVE
A3
1 CONROY CT
2 Westfield Trad Est
3 CRUIKSHANK'S CT
PO
2
SUTHERLAND DR
ARGYLL PATH
Denny High Sch
RAES VIEW
NETHERMAINS RD
WOODLAND WAY
REEDLANDS DR
HEATHERDALE GDNS
Chacefield Wood
HILLHOUSE RD
AFTON DR
GLENBO DR
GIBBDUN PL
1
OTHILL RD
LEITH PL
GARVALD RD
SOLWAY DR
HILLCREST PL
LAXDALE DR
CHACEFIELD WOOD
A872
FK4
GLOWRORUM DR
HAYFIELD TERR
ENDRICK DR
DROVE LOAN CRES
DROVE LOAN
HOME FARM COTTS
81
Head of Muir
Head of Muir Prim Sch
EARN PL
M876
HAYPARK RD
81
A
25
B
82
C
26
DENNY RD
URE CRES
CHACEFIELD ST
HEATLANDS AVE
BALFOUR ST
SPENCE ST
SKENE ST
ASHLEY ST
DUNCAIRN AVE
COWAN ST
HOPEPARK TERR
FAIRFIELD AVE
PEATHILL RD
LOMOND WAY
ANNET RD
BANKHEAD CRES
LOANHEAD AVE
PARK AVE
BANKVIEW TERR
Bankhead
MORRISON AVE
GLENMORE DR
ALLOWAY CRES

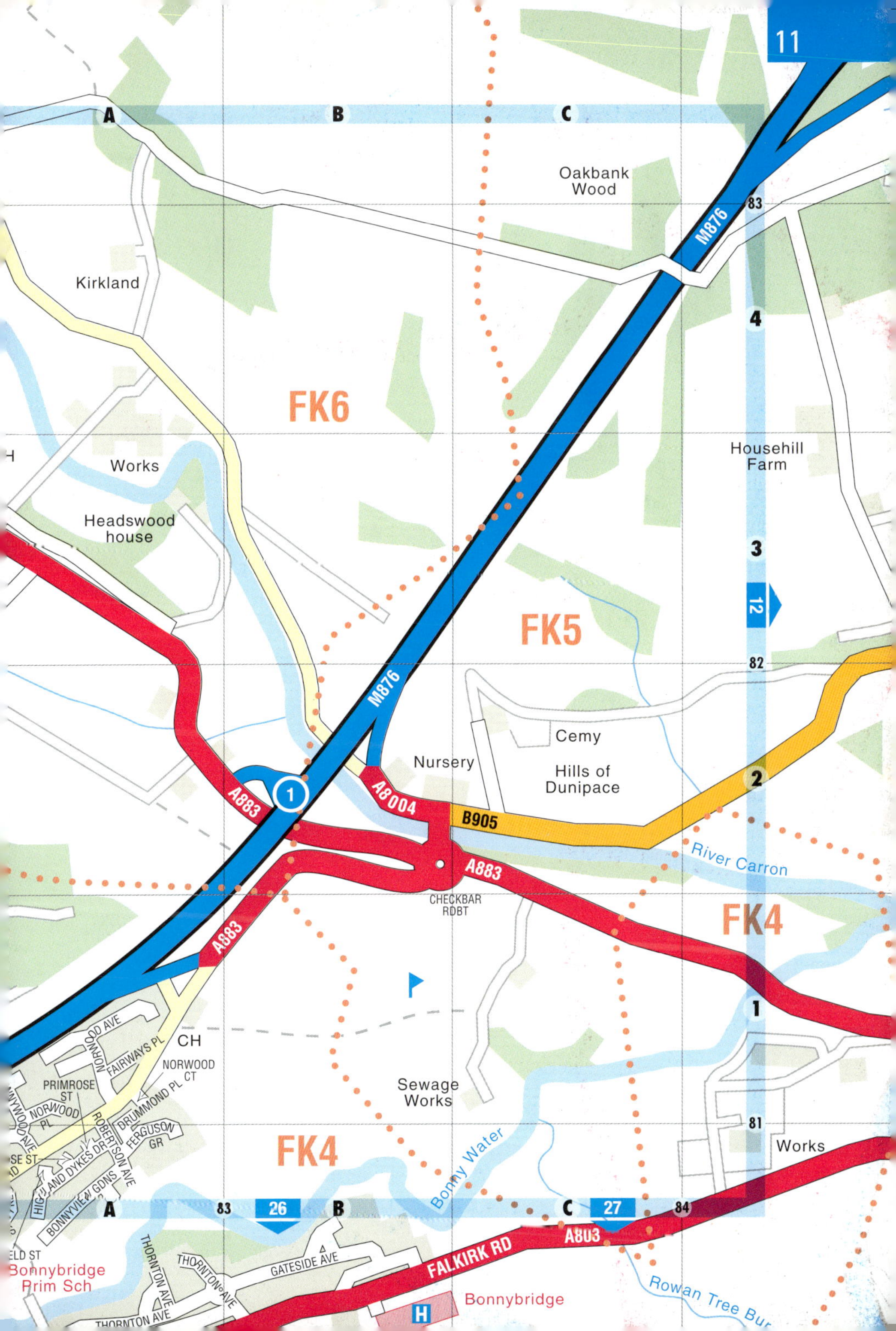
A
B
C
Oakbank
Wood
83
M876
Kirkland
4
FK6
Works
Householl
Farm
Headswood
house
3
12
FK5
82
M876
Cemy
Nursery
Hills of
Dunipace
1
A883
A8004
B905
2
River Carron
A883
CHECKBAR
RDBT
FK4
A883
1
CH
NORWOOD AVE
FAIRWAYS PL
NORWOOD
CT
PRIMROSE
ST
NORWOOD
PL
DRUMMOND PL
ROBERTSON DR
FERGUSON
GR
Sewage
Works
81
Works
FK4
Bonny Water
A
83
26
B
C
27
84
BONNYVIEW GDNS
ROBERTSON AVE
A803
FALKIRK RD
THORNTON AVE
GATESIDE AVE
Bonnybridge
Prim Sch
Bonnybridge
H
THORNTON AVE

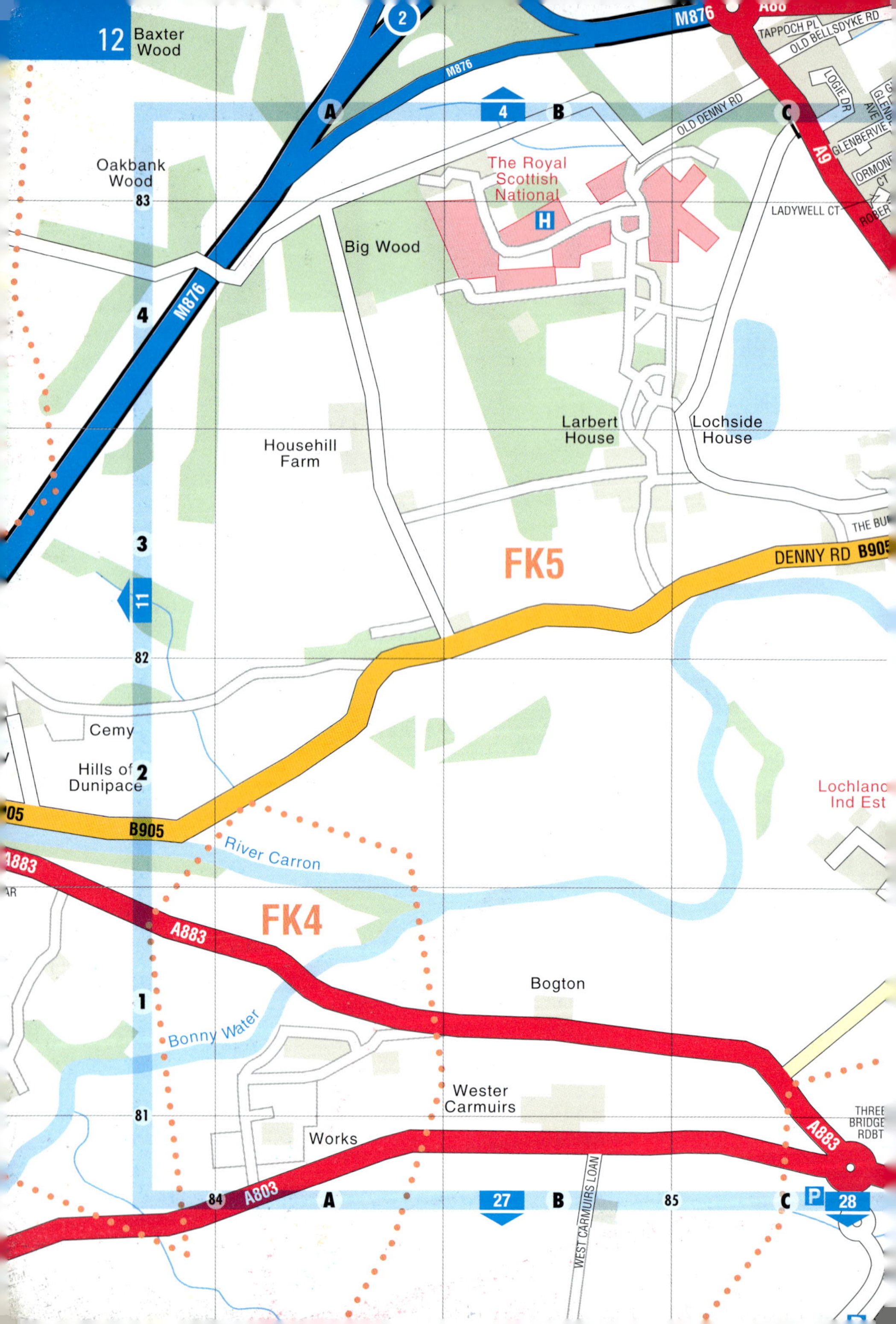
Baxter Wood
M876
A88
TAPPOCH PL
OLD BELLSDYKE RD
LOGIE DR
GLENBERVIE
OLD DENNY RD
A9
A
4
B
C
Oakbank Wood
83
The Royal Scottish National
H
LADYWELL CT
Big Wood
4
Larbert House
Lochside House
Househill Farm
THE BU
3
FK5
DENNY RD B905
11
82
Cemy
Hills of Dunipace
2
Lochland Ind Est
B905
River Carron
A883
FK4
Bogton
1
Bonny Water
Wester Carmuirs
THREE BRIDGE RDBT
81
Works
A883
A803
84
A
27
B
WEST CARMUIRS LOAN
85
C
P
28

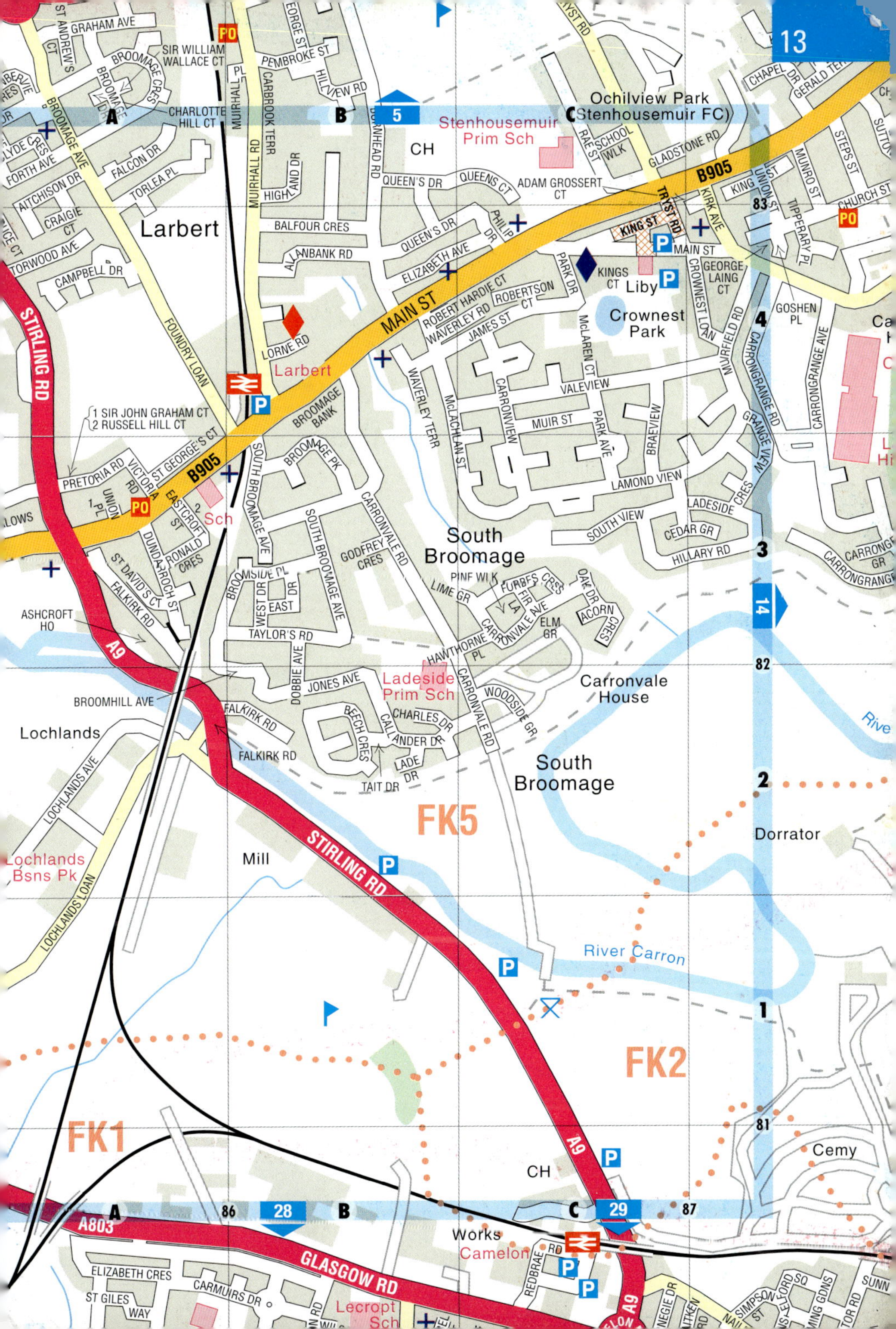
Larbert
South Broomage
Ochilview Park (Stenhousemuir FC)
Stenhousemuir Prim Sch
Crownest Park
Liby
Carronvale House
Ladeside Prim Sch
Lochlands
Lochlands Bsns Pk
Mill
Dorrator
River Carron
FK5
FK2
FK1
Cemy
Works
Camelon
Lecropt Sch
MAIN ST
B905
STIRLING RD
A9
GLASGOW RD
A803
FOUNDRY LOAN
BROOMAGE AVE
MUIRHALL RD
CARRONVALE RD
CARRONGRANGE RD
LOCHLANDS LOAN
LOCHLANDS AVE
FALKIRK RD
1 SIR JOHN GRAHAM CT
2 RUSSELL HILL CT
5
14
28
29
83
82
81
86
87

KING ST
PO
CHRISTIE TERR
JOHNSTON AVE
KINNAIRD DR
OCHIL DR
CHAPEL DR
GERALD TERR
LOCHABER DR
JAMIESON AVE
SCHOOL WLK
RAE ST
GLADSTONE RD
B905
TRYST RD
KING ST
MAIN ST
KIRK AVE
UNION ST
MUNRO ST
STEPS ST
TIPPERARY PL
CHURCH ST
AKARIT RD
SUTTON PARK CRES
SHERRIFF LA
BRUART AVE
ARTHUR'S DR
BRUCE DR
MEREDITH DR
KINGSLEY AVE
BARRIE RD
BARRIE RD
TWAIN AVE
FLEMING DR
BRONTE PL
ALLOA RD
MAPLE AVE
CUNNINGHAM RD
LARCH GR
CHESTNUT GR
ROSE TERR
ASH GR
HOLLY AVE
LODGE DR
CASTLE DR
CASTLE DR
ADAM CRES
STENHOUSE RD
NEW CARRON RD
B902
CARRICK PL
ARDVRECK PL
TANTALLON DR
ROUGHLAN
HERITAGE DR
BEAUFORT DR
CORTACHY AVE
ALLOA RD
CRAIGIEVAR
Carron Prim Sch
ALLOA RD
MACLAREN TERR
OCHIL TERR
PARK CR
Carron Bsn
CARRONLEA DR
CARRON RDBT
GROVE CRES
STEWART AVE
Carron
STENHOUSE RD
BURDER PK
ADAMS LOAN
SINCLAIR PL
Housemuir Prim Sch
PHILIP DR
KINGS CT
Liby
P
ROBERTSON CT
PARK DR
GEORGE LAING CT
CROWNEST LOAN
Crownest Park
McLAREN CT
MUIRFIELD RD
CARRONGRANGE RD
GOSHEN PL
CARRONGRANGE AVE
Carron Hill
FK5
Carrongrange Sch
Larbert High Sch
Carron Dams
Works
VALEVIEW
CARRONVIEW
MUIR ST
PARK AVE
BRAEVIEW
GRANGE VIEW
LAMOND VIEW
LADESIDE CRES
SOUTH VIEW
CEDAR GR
HILLARY RD
CARRONGRANGE GR
CARRONGRANGE GDNS
CANNONS WAY
PARK RD
PARK RD
SANFORD CRES
WILLIAMSON AVE
YARDLEY PL
SWORD'S WAY
JARVIE PL
CARRON RD
FARM ST
RIVER ST
MILLFLATTS ST
FORBES CRES
FIR LA
CARRONVALE AVE
ELM GR
13
C2
1 MULLOCH AVE
2 ANDERSON AVE
3 NEWCARRON CT
4 WILLIAMSON AVE
5 DUNDEE CT
6 JARVIE PL
7 JOHNSTON CT
8 GASCOIGNE CT
Carronvale House
WOODSIDE GR
River Carron
BUCHANAN CT
CONNER AVE
GRANARY RD
DUNDEE PL
MULLOCH AVE
COTLAND DR
MUIRHEAD AVE
WATERFURS DR
B906
B902
CARRON RD
Mungal
RONADES RD
Longdales
Dorrator
BROWNIEKNOWE PL 1
GOOSEDUBS PL 2
STEPHENS CROFT 3
CROFTHEAD ST
COTLAND DR
LONGDALES AVE
LONGDALES PL
LONGDALES CT
LONGDALES RD
VALLEYVIEW DR
VALLEYVIEW PL
ELLIOT TERR
BAIRNS FORD CT
BAIRNS FORD DR
BAIRNS FORD AVE
FK2
Mungal Farm
Crem
MERCHISTON TERR
MUNGALHEAD RD
GIBSONGRAY ST
NAPIER PL
NAPIER CRES
DOLLAR AVE
DOLLAR GDNS
Cauldhame
MERCHISTON RD
MERCHISTON AVE
MERCHISTON GDNS
MERCHISTON RDBT
A9
CH
CENTURION WAY
Cemy
FK1
St Francis Xavier's RC Prim Sch
St Mungo's High Sch
Grahams
REDBRAE RD
REDBRAE
SIMPSON ST
ELFORD SQ
SUNNYSIDE ST
TOR RD
MERCHISTON RD
A9
83
82
81
87
88
A
B
C
4
3
2
1
6
29
30

15
Carronshore
Westertown
Carron House
FK2
River Carron
FALKIRK
Langlees
Bainsford
Works
Bankside
Forth and Clyde Canal
FK2
A9
M9
B902
16
7
30
31
Langlees Prim Sch
Bainsford Prim Sch
Merchiston Ind Est
Castlelaurie Ind Est
Bankside Ind Est
Enterprise Pk
Middlefield Ind Est
Etna Ct
Bryson Street Ind Est
Victoria Prim Sch
Forth Valley Coll Falkirk
ABBOTS ROAD RDBT
MUNGALEND RDBT
ETNA ROAD RDBT
CARRONSHORE RD
BOTHKENNAR RD
WESTERTON TERR
MAIN ST
THE AVENUE
DAVID'S LOAN
ABBOTS RD
ETNA RD
MIDDLEFIELD RD
HAMS RD

Prim Sch
PO
Skinflats
8
A
B
C
BOTHKENNAR RD
TERR
POTTER PL
ZETLAND PL
CORONATION PL
NEWTON AVE
Backrow Farm
83
Carron House
VENUE
EDWARD PL
CAMPIE TERR
BINNIE PL
A905
M9
NEWTON RD
4
Yonderhaugh
River Carron
Glensburgh
3
FK2
Sewage Works
DEVON ST
BANK ST
AVON ST
DON ST
TWEED ST
KELVIN
TAY ST
DAVID'S LOAN
15
ABBOTS RD
82
DALGRAIN RD
6
ZETLAND DR
GLENSBURGH RD
Hotel
2
ABBOTS ROAD RDBT
A9
FK3
nkside Ind Est
CASTLE CRES
CASTLE PL
Enterprise Pk
West Mains Ind Est
WEST MAINS RD
EARL'S GATE RDBT
ETNA ROAD RDBT
ALMOND RD
ALMOND CT
THE ROUNDEL
ABBOTS RD
ABBOTS CT
1
West Mains Ind Est
A904
FALKIRK RD
Grangemouth Ent Ctr
Etna Ct
UNIVERSAL RD
COLLEGE CRES
HAZEL GR
81
CASTINGS CT
CASTINGS RD
YORK ST
FORBES CT
MIDDLEFIELD RD
90
A
31
B
91
C
32
LAURIESTON RD
ADAM ST
Middlefield
Victoria Prim Sch
Forth Valley Coll Falkirk
Valley Coll Falkirk
WESTFIELD RDBT
Falkirk Stadium

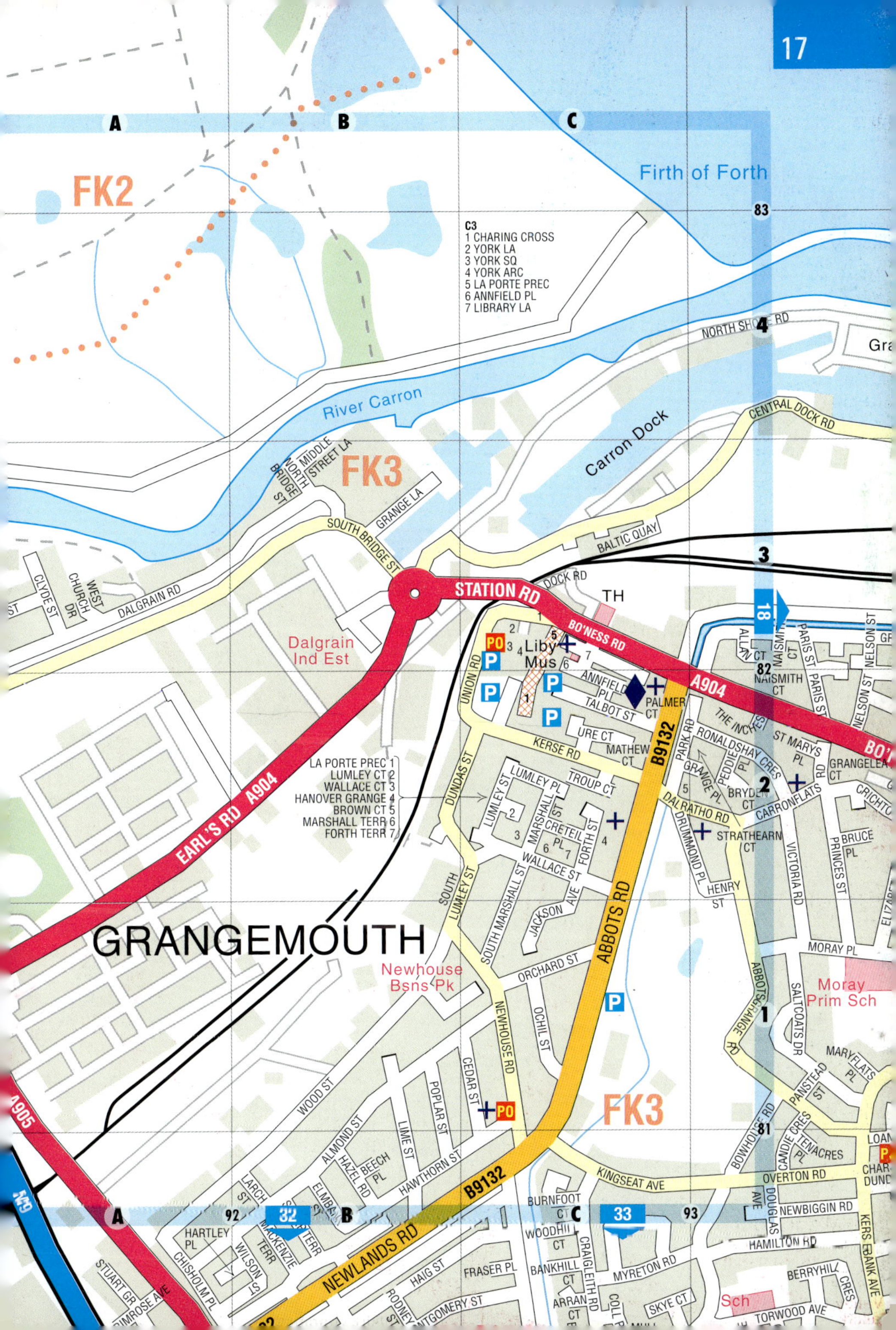

Firth of Forth
FK2
FK3
River Carron
Carron Dock
C3
1 CHARING CROSS
2 YORK LA
3 YORK SQ
4 YORK ARC
5 LA PORTE PREC
6 ANNFIELD PL
7 LIBRARY LA
LA PORTE PREC 1
LUMLEY CT 2
WALLACE CT 3
HANOVER GRANGE 4
BROWN CT 5
MARSHALL TERR 6
FORTH TERR 7
GRANGEMOUTH
Dalgrain Ind Est
Newhouse Bsns Pk
Moray Prim Sch
Liby
Mus
TH
Sch
STATION RD
BO'NESS RD
A904
EARL'S RD
A905
B9132
ABBOTS RD
NEWLANDS RD
SOUTH BRIDGE ST
DALGRAIN RD
CENTRAL DOCK RD
BALTIC QUAY
DOCK RD
NORTH SHORE RD
KERSE RD
DALRATHO RD
KINGSEAT AVE
OVERTON RD
HAMILTON RD
TORWOOD AVE
18
32
33

A
B
C
Firth of Forth
83
4
River Carron
NORTH SHORE RD
Grangemouth Harbour & Docks
Grange Dock
Western Channel
Carron Dock
CENTRAL DOCK RD
LC
FK3
BALTIC QUAY
3
DOCK RD
1 BELL CT
2 TAYLOR CT
3 NELSON GDNS
Grange Burn
LC's
SOUTH SHORE RD
BO'NESS RD
17
PO
Liby
Mus
82
ANNFIELD PL
TALBOT ST
PALMER CT
A904
ALLAN CT
NAISMITH CT
PARIS ST
NELSON ST
GRANGEBURN RD
ROXBURGH ST
GEORGE ST
KINGS RD
QUEEN ST
ALBERT AVE
POWDRAKE RD
WEST GATE RD
6TH ST
OLD REFINERY RD
CANDIE RD
3RD ST
2ND ST
1ST ST
URE CT
KERSE RD
MATHEW CT
B9132
PARK RD
THE INCHES
RONALDSHAY CRES
ST MARYS PL
GRANGELEA CT
GREEN LA
CRICHTON DR
OSWALD AVE
LUMLEY ST
LUMLEY PL
TROUP CT
2
MARSHALL ST
CRETEIL PL
FORTH ST
GRANGE PL
PEDDIE PL
BRYDEN CT
CARRONFLATS RD
DALRATHO RD
DRUMMOND PL
STRATHEARN CT
BRUCE PL
PRINCES ST
VICTORIA RD
ELIZABETH AVE
AVONDHU GDNS
DUKE ST
WALLACE ST
SOUTH MARSHALL ST
JACKSON AVE
ABBOTS RD
HENRY ST
HAWING PL
ABBOTSINCH RD
ABBOTSINCH CT
MORAY PL
OXGANG RD
ORCHARD ST
Moray Prim Sch
Abbotsinch Ind Est
WEST ERTON RD
NEWHOUSE RD
OCHIL ST
1
ABBOTSGRANGE RD
SALTCOATS DR
1 BEARCROFT GDNS
2 ABERCAIRNEY PL
3 OLDWALLS PL
MARYFLATS PL
FENDOCH RD
STROWAN RD
STROWAN SQ
B9143
INCHYRA RD
PANSTEAD ST
WESTERTON RD
INCHYRA PL
81
BOWHOUSE RD
CANDIE CRES
TENACRES PL
LOANHEAD AVE
JAMES CORNWALL CT
YARROW PL
KINGSEAT AVE
OVERTON RD
CHARLOTTE DUNDAS CT
AMBERLEY PATH
ROAD 17
ROAD 21
BURNFOOT CT
WOODHILL CT
93
DOUGLAS AVE
NEWIGGIN RD
KERSIEBANK AVE
AVONBANK AVE
33
DRYBURGH WAY
94
34
ROAD 24
CASTLETON CRES
HAMILTON RD
BANKHILL CT
CRAIGLEITH RD
MYRETON RD
ARRAN CT
SKYE CT
BERRYHILL CRES
CLARET RD
Sch
TORWOOD AVE

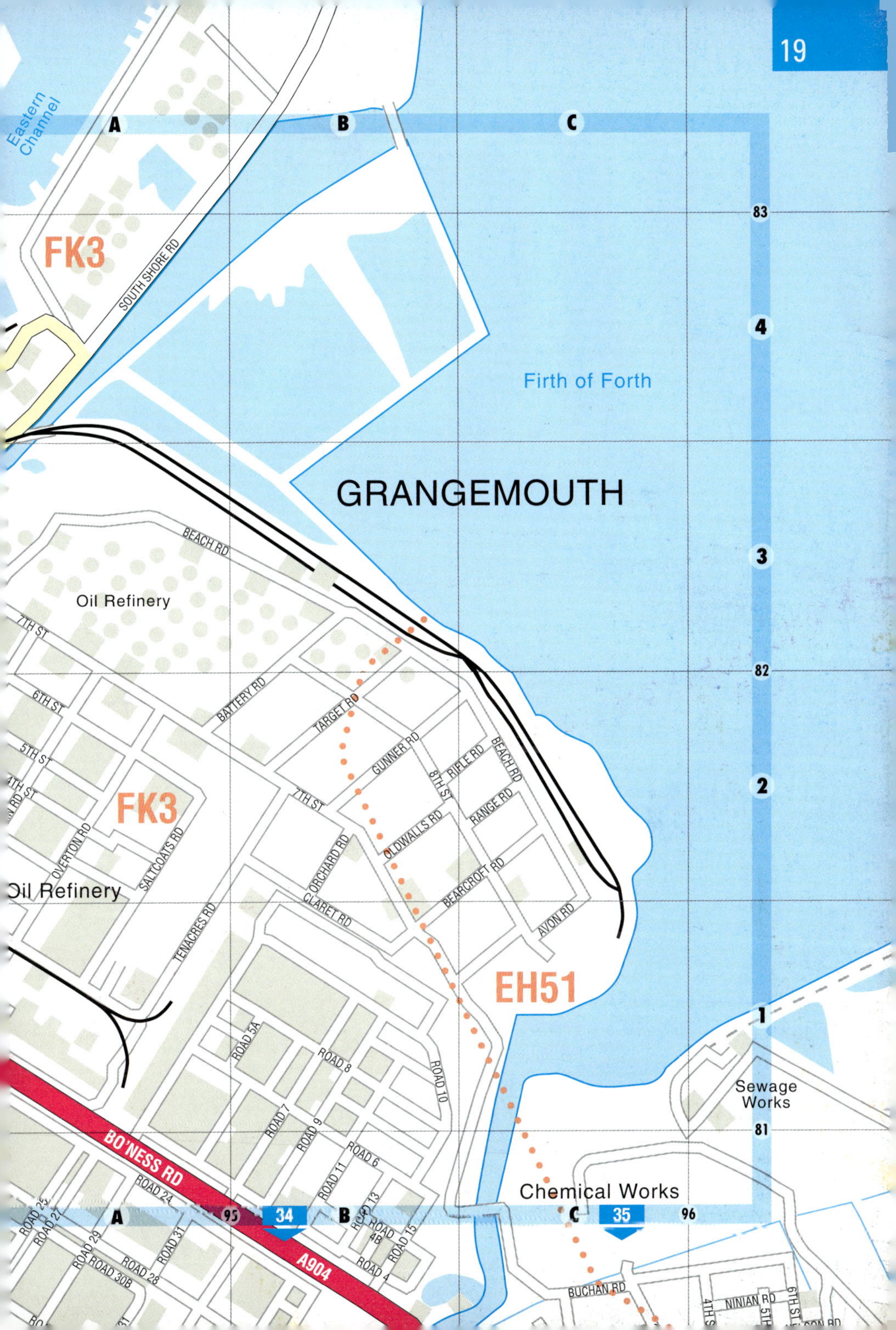

Eastern Channel
A
B
C
83
4
3
82
2
1
81
FK3
SOUTH SHORE RD
Firth of Forth
GRANGEMOUTH
BEACH RD
Oil Refinery
7TH ST
6TH ST
5TH ST
4TH ST
3RD ST
BATTERY RD
TARGET RD
GUNNER RD
8TH ST
RIFLE RD
BEACH RD
FK3
7TH ST
OVERTON RD
SALTCOATS RD
RANGE RD
OLDWALLS RD
ORCHARD RD
Oil Refinery
CLARET RD
BEARCROFT RD
AVON RD
TENACRES RD
EH51
ROAD 5A
ROAD 8
ROAD 10
Sewage Works
ROAD 7
ROAD 9
BO'NESS RD
ROAD 6
ROAD 11
ROAD 24
Chemical Works
ROAD 23
ROAD 21
95
34
ROAD 13
35
96
ROAD 29
ROAD 31
ROAD 4B
ROAD 15
ROAD 30B
ROAD 28
A904
ROAD 4
BUCHAN RD
NINIAN RD
4TH ST
5TH ST
6TH ST

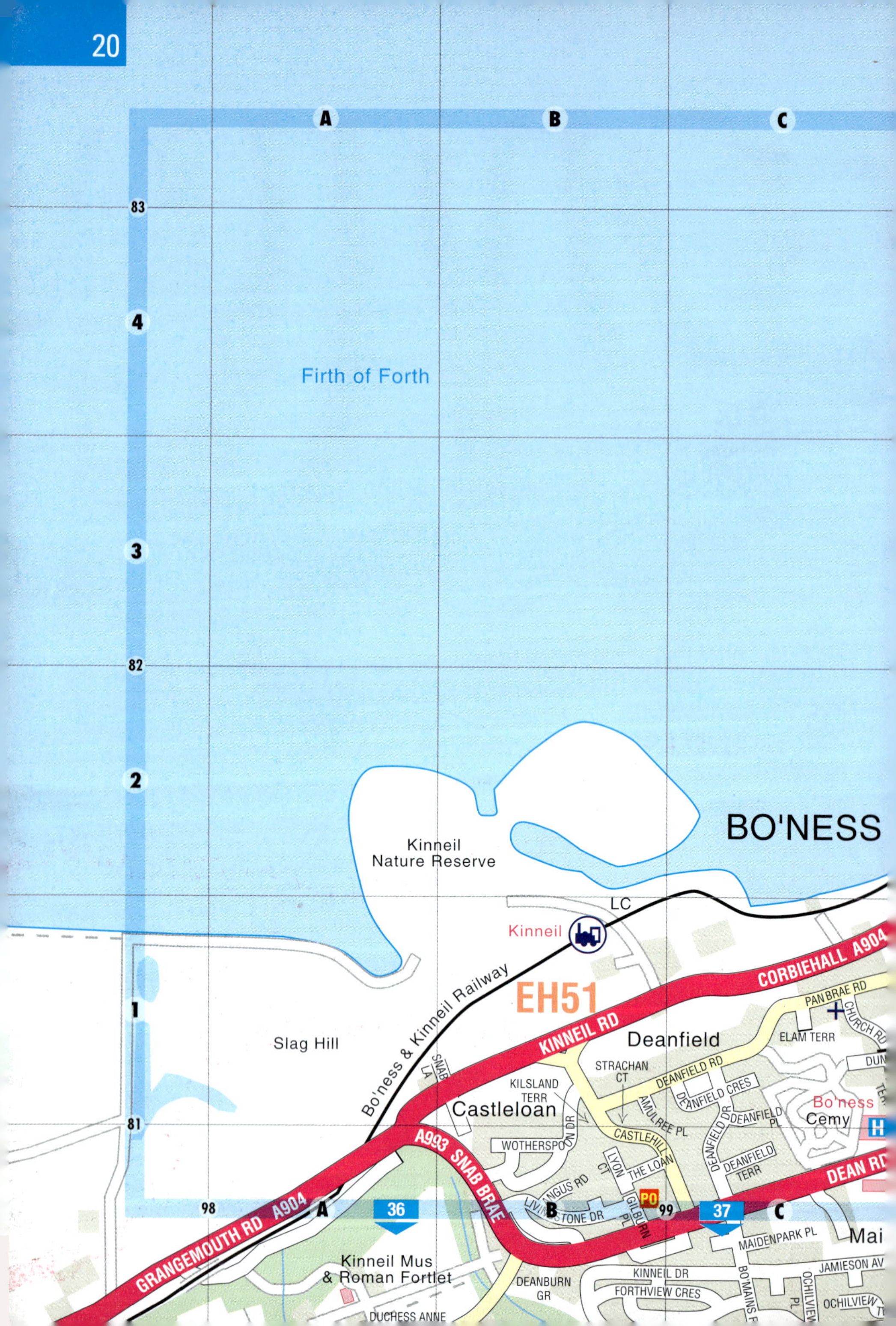

A
B
C
83
4
Firth of Forth
3
82
2
BO'NESS
Kinneil
Nature Reserve
LC
Kinneil
Bo'ness & Kinneil Railway
EH51
CORBIEHALL A904
PAN BRAE RD
CHURCH RD
1
Slag Hill
KINNEIL RD
Deanfield
ELAM TERR
STRACHAN CT
DEANFIELD RD
KILSLAND TERR
DEANFIELD CRES
Castleloan
AMULREE PL
DEANFIELD DR
DEANFIELD PL
Bo'ness
Cemy
81
CASTLEHILL
A993 SNAB BRAE
WOTHERSPOON DR
LYON CT
THE LOAN
DEANFIELD TERR
DEAN RD
ANGUS RD
PO
98
GRANGEMOUTH RD A904
A
36
B
LIVINGSTONE DR
GILBURN PL
99
37
C
MAIDENPARK PL
Mai
Kinneil Mus
& Roman Fortlet
KINNEIL DR
JAMIESON AV
DEANBURN GR
FORTHVIEW CRES
OCHILVIEW
DUCHESS ANNE

Firth of Forth
West Pier
SCOTLANDS CL 1
UNION ST 2
EAST PIER ST 3
REGISTER ST 4
MARKET ST 5
HAMILTON LA 6
HOPE ST 7
PROVIDENCE BRAE 8
MARCHLANDS TERR 9
1 UNION CT
2 OLD ST MARY'S LA
Bo'ness & Kinneil Railway
Scottish Railway Exhibition
Bo'ness
3 MAN O' WAR WAY
4 THIRLESTANE PL
UNION ST
DOCK ST
LINKS RD
GRANGEPANS
A904
A706
A993
Grangepans
1 MARCHLANDS TERR
2 MARCHLANDS LA
EH51
DEAN RD
St Mary's RC Prim Sch
Bo'ness Acad
Grange Prim Sch
Newtown
Mingle
Kinneil Prim Sch
GRAHAMSDYKE RD
LINLITHGOW RD
Mus
Kinninga
Drum
22
37
38
83
82
81
00
01

A
B
C
83
4
3
21
82
2
1
81
01
02
38
39
Firth of Forth
Bridgeness
Mus
Victoria Mills Ind Est
Carriden Ind Est
PIER RD
THIRLESTANE
DOWER CRES
HANEY'S WAY
GRANGEPANS
A904
PO
VICTORIA PL
PARK LA
LINKS
CAIRN'S LA
RATTRAY ST
DOOCOT BRAE
COWDENHILL RD
CRAIG VIEW
PHILPINGSTONE RD
BRIDGENESS CRES
THE TOWER GDNS
BRIDGENESS LA
BRIDGENESS RD
SOUTH PHILPINGSTONE LA
HARBOUR RD
1 THE RUN
2 PHILPINGSTONE LA
3 FURNACE LA
GRANGE TERR
GRAHAMSDYKE AVE
Grange Prim Sch
GRANGE LOAN
FOUNTAINPARK CRES
Carriden
KINACRES GR
FOREDALE TERR
CUFFABOUTS
CARRIDEN GLADE
BO'NESS
Kinningars Park
EH51
Old Manse Wood
GRAHAMSDYKE TERR
GRAHAM CRES
SETON TERR
A993
DRUMSIDE TERR
Drum
DRUM COTTS
MARYFIELD DR
The Old Manse
Cat Craig
Carriden Burn
A904
CARRIDEN BRAE
HADRIAN WAY
DRUMPARK AVE
DRUM RD
MUIRHOUSES SQ
DRUMACRE RD
MUIREND CT
GRAHAMSDYKE RD
ACRE RD
GLENARD VIEW

Glenhead
Drumbowie Resr
FK6
Bowridge
Easter Kelt
KELT RD
Easter Wairds
Braeface
Wester Banknock
24
Wester Thomaston
FK4
M80
Cloybank
Doups Burn
Hotel
Banknock
HOLLANDBUSH AVE
BRAEFACE RD
KILSYTH RD
A803 Kilsyth
A80
JOHN ST
A803
KILSYTH
Bankier Prim Sch
HOLLANDBUSH CRES
BANKIER TERR
KERR CRES
JAMES ST
VIEWFIELD RD
JOHN BASSY DR
BOG RD
BANKIER RD
BALLINKIER AVE
CASTLEVIEW TERR
GARNGREW RD
MARGARET AVE
GLENVIEW AVE
HILLHEAD AVE
CUMBERNAULD RD
Bog
Haggs
LABURNUM RD
MAPLE PL
AUCHINCLOCH DR
LINDEN DR
ROWAN DR
ASH PL
KELVINVIEW AVE
CASTLEHILL CRES
LAUREL SQ
WELLPARK RD
WILLOW DR
HAWTHORN DR
HOLLY GR
Castlecary Mill Farm
CEDAR RD
A80 Cumbernauld (A8011)
Forth & Clyde Canal
LARCH DR
ALMOND DR
HAZEL RD
A
B
C
1
2
3
4
78
79
80
81
PO

Little Denny Reservoir
M80
A
B
9
C
Whitehill
MYOTHILL RD
Drumbowie Resr
81
Easter Kelt
KELT RD
4
FK6
Mast
Easter Banknock
Wester Bankhead
5
Banknock
3
Wester Banknock
23
80
2
M80
STATION RD
McVEAN PL
GLASGOW RD
WATSON PL
Parkfoot
4
Longcroft
ANDERSON TERR
MAYFIELD DR
No 1 Holding
A80
A80
JOHN ST
KILSYTH RD
A803
CROFT EST
Longcroft Farm
1
PO
KERR CRES
JAMES ST
GARNGREW RD
CASTLEVIEW TERR
CUMBERNAULD RD
MARGARET AVE
GLENVIEW AVE
Haggs
LONGCROFT HOLDINGS
FK4
Underwood Farm
79
Underwood House
Forth & Clyde Canal
Castlecary Mill Farm
79
A
B
80
C
B816
THORNDALE GDNS
PO
ALLANDALE COTTS

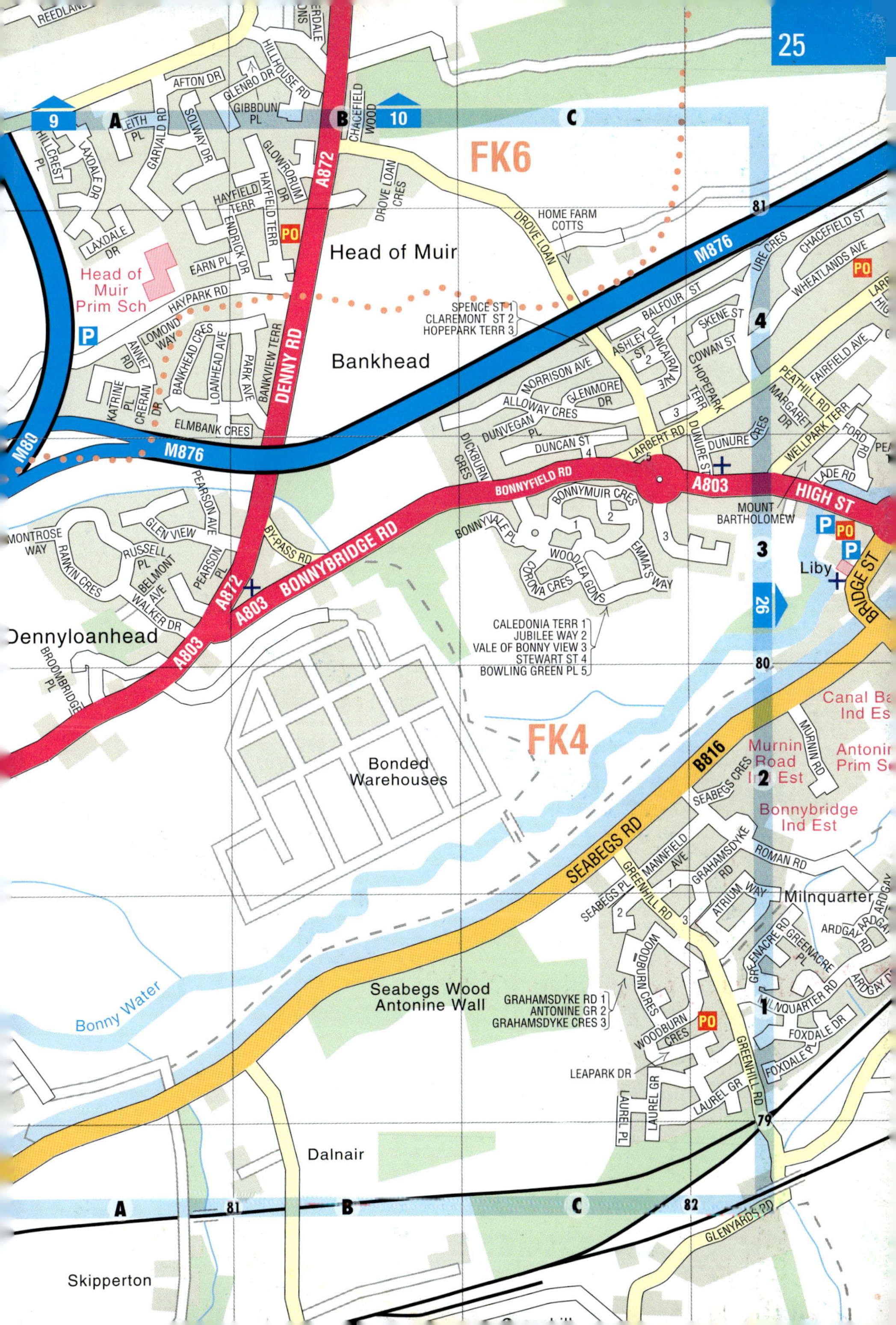

REEDLANDS
HILLHOUSE RD
AFTON DR
GLENBO DR
GIBBDUN PL
9
A
LEITH PL
B
10
CHACEFIELD WOOD
C
HILLCREST PL
LAXDALE DR
GARVALD RD
SOLWAY DR
GLOWRORUM DR
A872
FK6
DROVE LOAN CRES
HAYFIELD TERR
ENDRICK DR
PO
HOME FARM COTTS
DROVE LOAN
81
LAXDALE DR
Head of Muir
M876
URE CRES
CHACEFIELD ST
WHEATLANDS AVE
Head of Muir Prim Sch
EARN PL
HAYPARK RD
SPENCE ST 1
CLAREMONT ST 2
HOPEPARK TERR 3
BALFOUR ST
SKENE ST
ASHLEY ST
DUNCAIRN AVE
COWAN ST
4
LOMOND WAY
ANNET RD
BANKHEAD CRES
LOANHEAD AVE
PARK AVE
BANKVIEW TERR
DENNY RD
Bankhead
MORRISON AVE
GLENMORE DR
HOPEPARK TERR
PEATHILL RD
FAIRFIELD AVE
MARGARET DR
KATRINE PL
CRERAN DR
ALLOWAY CRES
DUNVEGAN PL
DUNURE ST
DUNURE CRES
WELLPARK TERR
FORD RD
ELMBANK CRES
LARBERT RD
M80
M876
DICKBURN CRES
DUNCAN ST
LADE RD
PEARSON AVE
BONNYFIELD RD
A803
HIGH ST
MOUNT BARTHOLOMEW
BONNYMUIR CRES
GLEN VIEW
MONTROSE WAY
RANKIN CRES
RUSSELL PL
BY-PASS RD
BONNYVALE PL
P
PO
3
BELMONT AVE
PEARSON PL
BONNYBRIDGE RD
WOODLEA GDNS
EMMA'S WAY
CORONA CRES
Liby
BRIDGE ST
26
WALKER DR
A872
A803
Dennyloanhead
A803
CALEDONIA TERR 1
JUBILEE WAY 2
VALE OF BONNY VIEW 3
STEWART ST 4
BOWLING GREEN PL 5
80
BROOMBRIDGE PL
Canal Ba Ind Es
FK4
Murnin Road Ind Est
MURNIN RD
Antonin Prim S
B816
SEABEGS CRES
2
Bonded Warehouses
Bonnybridge Ind Est
SEABEGS RD
MANNFIELD AVE
GRAHAMSDYKE RD
ROMAN RD
GREENHILL RD
ATRIUM WAY
Milnquarter
SEABEGS PL
GREENACRE RD
GREENACRE PL
ARDGAY RD
Seabegs Wood Antonine Wall
WOODBURN CRES
GRAHAMSDYKE RD 1
ANTONINE GR 2
GRAHAMSDYKE CRES 3
MILNQUARTER RD
1
Bonny Water
WOODBURN CRES
PO
FOXDALE DR
FOXDALE PL
LEAPARK DR
GREENHILL RD
LAUREL GR
LAUREL PL
79
Dalnair
A
81
B
C
82
GLENYARDS RD
Skipperton

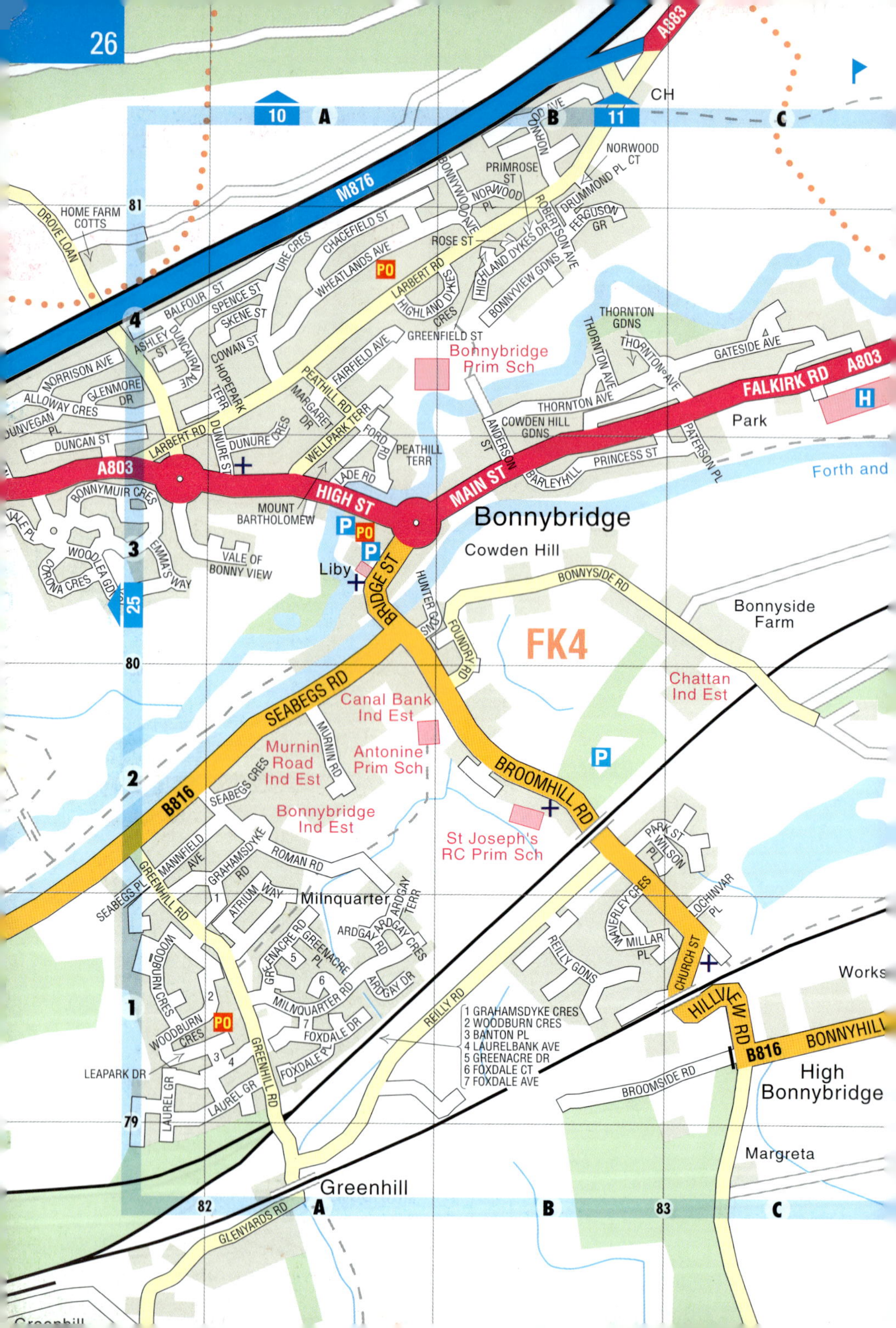

10
11
25
A
B
C
CH
M876
A883
A803
B816
FK4
Bonnybridge
Cowden Hill
High Bonnybridge
Milnquarter
Greenhill
Park
Works
Margreta
Bonnyside Farm
Forth and
HOME FARM COTTS
DROVE LOAN
NORWOOD AVE
NORWOOD CT
NORWOOD PL
PRIMROSE ST
DRUMMOND PL
FERGUSON GR
ROBERTSON AVE
ROSE ST
HIGHLAND DYKES DR
HIGHLAND DYKES CRES
BONNYVIEW GDNS
BONNYWOOD AVE
CHACEFIELD ST
WHEATLANDS AVE
URE CRES
LARBERT RD
GREENFIELD ST
BALFOUR ST
SPENCE ST
SKENE ST
COWAN ST
ASHLEY ST
DUNCAIRN AVE
HOPEPARK TERR
NORRISON AVE
GLENMORE DR
ALLOWAY CRES
DUNVEGAN PL
DUNCAN ST
DUNURE ST
DUNURE CRES
PEATHILL RD
MARGARET DR
FAIRFIELD AVE
WELLPARK TERR
FORD RD
PEATHILL TERR
LADE RD
MOUNT BARTHOLOMEW
HIGH ST
MAIN ST
FALKIRK RD
BONNYMUIR CRES
WOODLEA GDNS
CORONA CRES
EMMA'S WAY
VALE OF BONNY VIEW
Bonnybridge Prim Sch
THORNTON GDNS
THORNTON AVE
GATESIDE AVE
COWDEN HILL GDNS
ANDERSON ST
BARLEYHILL
PRINCESS ST
PATERSON PL
Liby
BRIDGE ST
HUNTER GDNS
FOUNDRY RD
BONNYSIDE RD
Chattan Ind Est
SEABEGS RD
Canal Bank Ind Est
Antonine Prim Sch
Murnin Road Ind Est
MURNIN RD
SEABEGS CRES
Bonnybridge Ind Est
BROOMHILL RD
St Joseph's RC Prim Sch
ROMAN RD
GRAHAMSDYKE RD
MANNFIELD AVE
SEABEGS PL
GREENHILL RD
ATRIUM WAY
ARDGAY TERR
ARDGAY RD
ARDGAY CRES
ARDGAY DR
GREENACRE RD
GREENACRE PL
MILNQUARTER RD
FOXDALE DR
FOXDALE PL
WOODBURN CRES
LEAPARK DR
LAUREL GR
PARK ST
WILSON PL
WAVERLEY CRES
LOCHINVAR PL
MILLAR PL
REILLY GDNS
CHURCH ST
REILLY RD
HILLVIEW RD
BONNYHILL
BROOMSIDE RD
GLENYARDS RD
1 GRAHAMSDYKE CRES
2 WOODBURN CRES
3 BANTON PL
4 LAURELBANK AVE
5 GREENACRE DR
6 FOXDALE CT
7 FOXDALE AVE
81
80
79
82
83

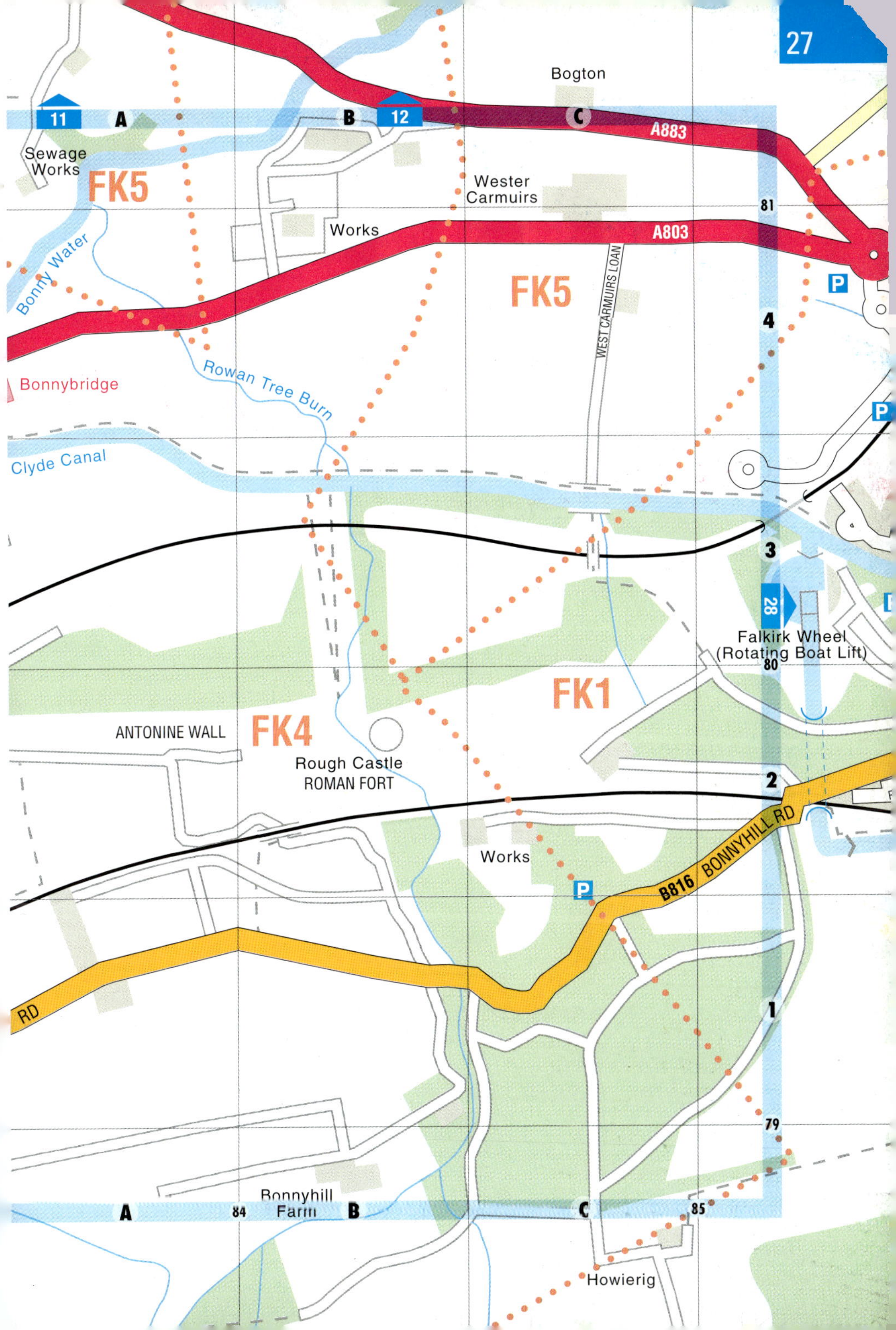
11
12
A
B
C
Bogton
A883
Sewage Works
FK5
Wester Carmuirs
Works
A803
81
Bonny Water
FK5
WEST CARMUIRS LOAN
4
P
Bonnybridge
Rowan Tree Burn
P
Clyde Canal
3
28
Falkirk Wheel (Rotating Boat Lift)
80
FK1
ANTONINE WALL
FK4
Rough Castle
ROMAN FORT
2
BONNYHILL RD
Works
P
B816
RD
1
79
Bonnyhill Farm
A
84
B
C
85
Howierig

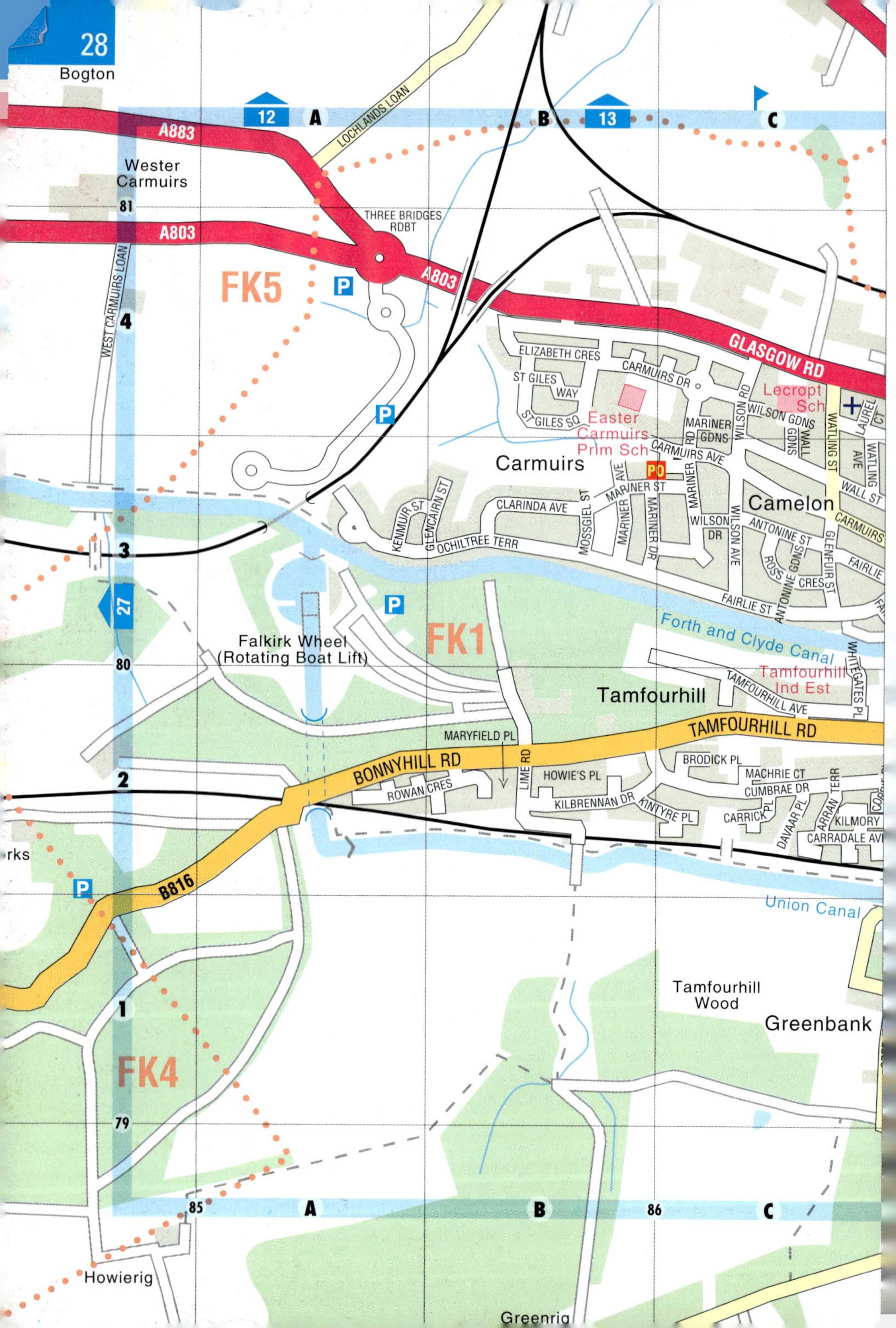
Bogton
12
13
A
B
C
A883
LOCHLANDS LOAN
Wester Carmuirs
81
A803
THREE BRIDGES RDBT
FK5
WEST CARMUIRS LOAN
4
GLASGOW RD
ELIZABETH CRES
ST GILES WAY
ST GILES SQ
CARMUIRS DR
Easter Carmuirs Prim Sch
Lecropt Sch
WILSON RD
WILSON GDNS
MARINER GDNS
CARMUIRS AVE
WATLING ST
LAUREL CT
WALL GDNS
WATLING AVE
WALL ST
Carmuirs
PO
MARINER ST
MARINER AVE
MARINER DR
MARINER RD
MOSSGIEL ST
CLARINDA AVE
KENMUIR ST
GLENCAIRN ST
OCHILTREE TERR
WILSON DR
WILSON AVE
Camelon
ANTONINE ST
ANTONINE GDNS
ROSS CRES
GLENFUIR ST
CARMUIRS
FAIRLIE
FAIRLIE ST
3
27
80
Falkirk Wheel (Rotating Boat Lift)
FK1
Forth and Clyde Canal
Tamfourhill Ind Est
WHITEGATES PL
Tamfourhill
TAMFOURHILL AVE
TAMFOURHILL RD
MARYFIELD PL
BONNYHILL RD
LIME RD
HOWIE'S PL
BRODICK PL
MACHRIE CT
CUMBRAE DR
ROWAN CRES
2
KILBRENNAN DR
KINTYRE PL
CARRICK PL
DAVAAR PL
ARRAN TERR
KILMORY
CARRADALE AVE
B816
Union Canal
Tamfourhill Wood
Greenbank
1
FK4
79
85
86
Howierig
Greenrig

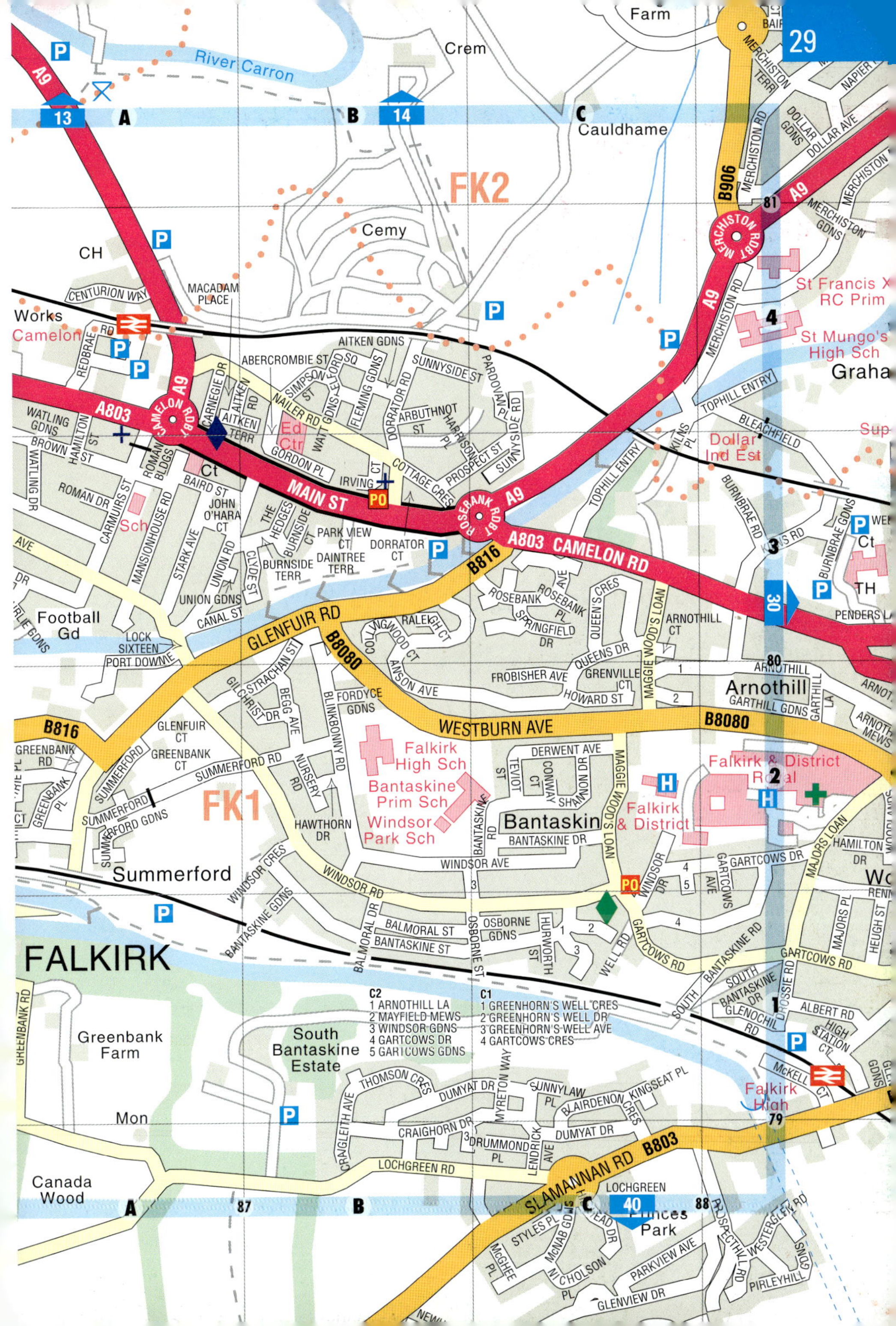

River Carron
Farm
Crem
Cauldhame
FK2
Cemy
CH
A9
13
14
A
B
C
B906
MERCHISTON TERR
MERCHISTON RD
DOLLAR GDNS
DOLLAR AVE
NAPIER
MERCHISTON RDBT
MERCHISTON GDNS
St Francis X RC Prim
St Mungo's High Sch
Graha
CENTURION WAY
MACADAM PLACE
Works
Camelon
REDBRAE RD
AITKEN GDNS
ABERCROMBIE ST
SQ
SUNNYSIDE ST
PARDOVAN PL
SUNNYSIDE RD
TOPHILL ENTRY
BLEACHFIELD
Dollar Ind Est
Sup
KILNS PL
A803
CAMELON RDBT
CARNEGIE DR
AITKEN RD
AITKEN TERR
NAILER RD
SIMPSON ST
ELFORD GDNS
WATT GDNS
FLEMING GDNS
DORRATOR RD
ARBUTHNOT ST
HARRISON PL
PROSPECT ST
Ed Ctr
GORDON PL
WATLING GDNS
HAMILTON ST
BROWN ST
WATLING DR
ROMAN BLDGS
Ct
BAIRD ST
ROMAN DR
CARMUIRS ST
Sch
MANSIONHOUSE RD
JOHN O'HARA CT
STARK AVE
UNION RD
THE HEDGES
BURNSIDE CT
MAIN ST
IRVING CT
COTTAGE CRES
PO
ROSEBANK RDBT
A803 CAMELON RD
BURNBRAE RD
KILNS RD
BURNBRAE GDNS
Ct
TH
WE
PENDERS LA
30
PARK VIEW CT
DORRATOR CT
DAINTREE TERR
BURNSIDE TERR
CLYDE ST
UNION GDNS
CANAL ST
B816
Football Gd
LOCK SIXTEEN
PORT DOWNIE
AVE
GLENFUIR RD
B8080
COLLINGWOOD CT
RALEIGH CT
ROSEBANK AVE
ROSEBANK PL
SPRINGFIELD DR
QUEEN'S CRES
MAGGIE WOOD'S LOAN
ARNOTHILL CT
ANSON AVE
FROBISHER AVE
QUEENS DR
GRENVILLE CT
HOWARD ST
ARNOTHILL
Arnothill
GARTHILL GDNS
GARTHILL LA
ARNOTHILL MEWS
STRACHAN ST
GILCHRIST DR
BEGG AVE
FORDYCE GDNS
BLINKBONNY RD
WESTBURN AVE
B8080
GLENFUIR CT
GREENBANK RD
GREENBANK CT
GREENBANK PL
SUMMERFORD
SUMMERFORD RD
SUMMERFORD GDNS
FK1
NURSERY RD
Falkirk High Sch
Bantaskine Prim Sch
Windsor Park Sch
HAWTHORN DR
TEVIOT ST
DERWENT AVE
CONWAY CT
SHANNON DR
BANTASKINE RD
Bantaskin
BANTASKINE DR
Falkirk & District
Falkirk & District Royal
HAMILTON DR
MAJORS LOAN
Summerford
WINDSOR CRES
WINDSOR RD
WINDSOR AVE
WINDSOR DR
GARTCOWS DR
GARTCOWS AVE
Wo
RENN
BANTASKINE GDNS
BALMORAL DR
BALMORAL ST
BANTASKINE ST
OSBORNE GDNS
OSBORNE ST
HURWORTH ST
WELL RD
GARTCOWS RD
BANTASKINE RD
MAJORS PL
HEUGH ST
FALKIRK
SOUTH BANTASKINE RD
SOUTH BANTASKINE DR
GLENOCHIL RD
DROSSIE RD
ALBERT RD
HIGH STATION CT
McKELL CT
Falkirk High
GREENBANK RD
Greenbank Farm
South Bantaskine Estate
C2
1 ARNOTHILL LA
2 MAYFIELD MEWS
3 WINDSOR GDNS
4 GARTCOWS DR
5 GARTCOWS GDNS
C1
1 GREENHORN'S WELL CRES
2 GREENHORN'S WELL DR
3 GREENHORN'S WELL AVE
4 GARTCOWS CRES
THOMSON CRES
DUMYAT DR
MYRETON WAY
SUNNYLAW PL
BLAIRDENON CRES
KINGSEAT PL
CRAIGLEITH AVE
CRAIGHORN DR
DRUMMOND PL
LENDRICK AVE
DUMYAT DR
B803
Mon
LOCHGREEN RD
SLAMANNAN RD
LOCHGREEN
Canada Wood
87
40
88
79
80
81
Princes Park
STYLES PL
McNAB GD
McGHEE PL
NICHOLSON PL
PARKVIEW AVE
GLENVIEW DR
WESTERGLEN RD
PIRLEYHILL GDNS

FK2
FK1
Grahamston
Arnothill
Woodlands
Cauldhame
Princes Park
Castlelaurie Ind Est
Forth and Clyde Canal
Bryson Street Ind Est
St Francis Xavier's RC Prim Sch
St Mungo's High Sch
Superstore
Dollar Ind Est
Firs Park (E Stirlingshire FC)
Central Ret Pk
Falkirk Grahamston
Liby
TH
Ct
Falkirk & District Royal
Falkirk & District
Prim Sch
Falkirk High
Ladysmill Ind Est
MAIN ST
GRAHAMS RD
CAMELON RD
WEST BRIDGE ST
TANNERS RD
WESTBURN AVE
KERSE LA
SLAMANNAN RD
GLEN BRAE
HIGH ST
MERCHISTON RDBT
GRAHAMS ROAD RDBT
LOCHGREEN RDBT
A9
A803
A904
B803
B902
B906
B8028
B8080
14
15
29
40
41
B3
1 SILK HO
2 MELVILLE ST
3 MELVILLE LA
4 SOUTH MELVILLE LA
5 Newmarket Ctr
6 UPPER NEWMARKET ST
7 NEWMARKET ST
WEE RD 1
WALLACE BLDGS 2
B2
1 BURNFOOT LA
2 KIRK WYND
3 TOLBOOTH ST
4 WOOER ST
5 Callendar Square Sh Ctr
6 Howgate Sh Ctr
7 KINGS CT
8 MISSION LA
9 MELROSE PL
10 ST ANDREWS PL
11 PLEASANCE SQ
12 PLEASANCE CT
13 ST MODANS CT
14 COMELY PARK TERR
15 BLUEBELL CL
16 WILSON'S CL
17 COMELY PARK GDNS
1 PARKFOOT CT
2 GLENBRAE CT

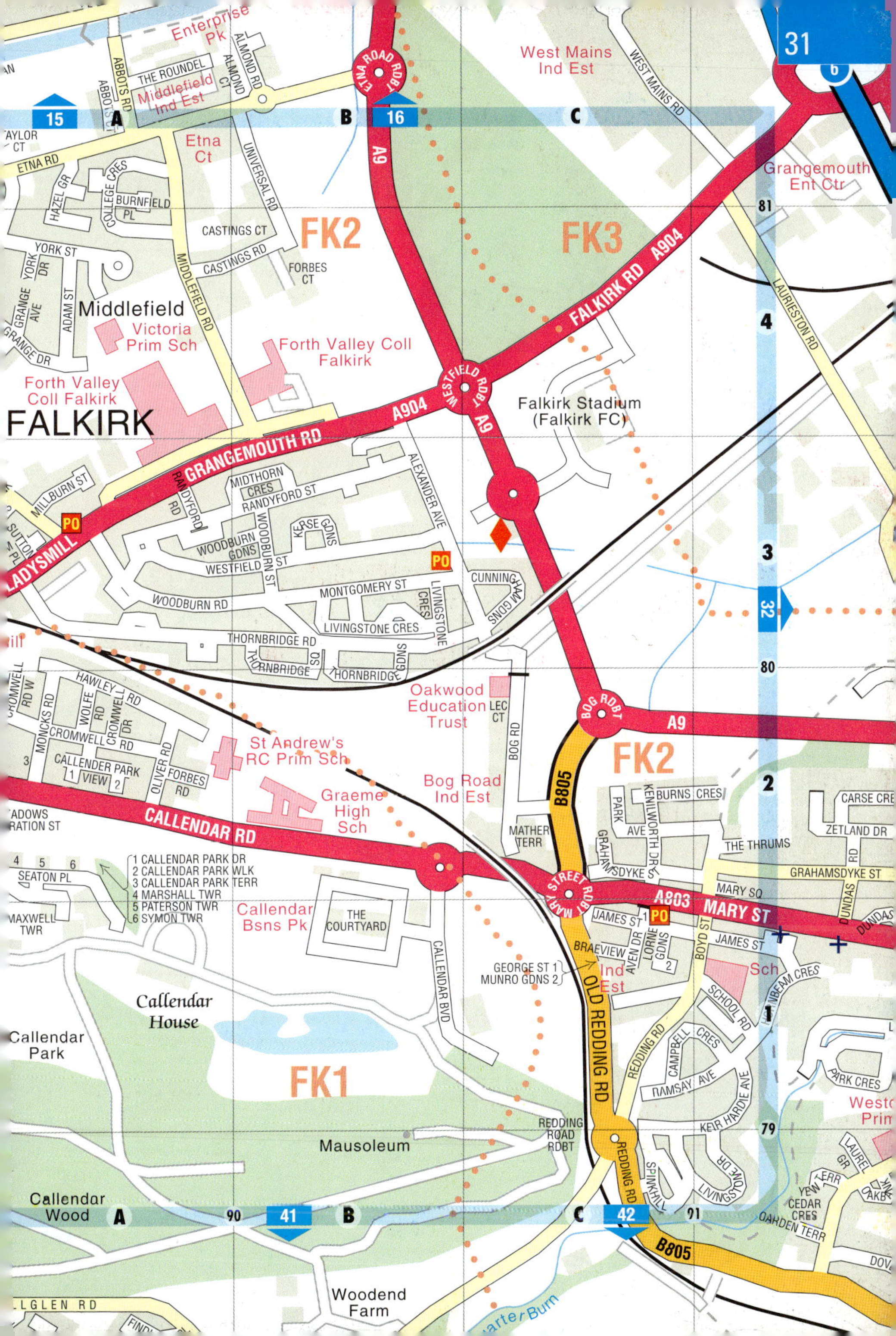
FALKIRK
Middlefield
FK1
FK2
FK3
Enterprise Pk
Middlefield Ind Est
Etna Ct
West Mains Ind Est
Grangemouth Ent Ctr
Victoria Prim Sch
Forth Valley Coll Falkirk
Falkirk Stadium (Falkirk FC)
Oakwood Education Trust
St Andrew's RC Prim Sch
Graeme High Sch
Bog Road Ind Est
Callendar Bsns Pk
Callendar House
Callendar Park
Mausoleum
Callendar Wood
Woodend Farm
GRANGEMOUTH RD
FALKIRK RD
CALLENDAR RD
MARY ST
OLD REDDING RD
WESTFIELD RDBT
ETNA ROAD RDBT
BOG RDBT
MARY STREET RDBT
REDDING ROAD RDBT
1 CALLENDAR PARK DR
2 CALLENDAR PARK WLK
3 CALLENDAR PARK TERR
4 MARSHALL TWR
5 PATERSON TWR
6 SYMON TWR
GEORGE ST 1
MUNRO GDNS 2
15
16
32
41
42
6

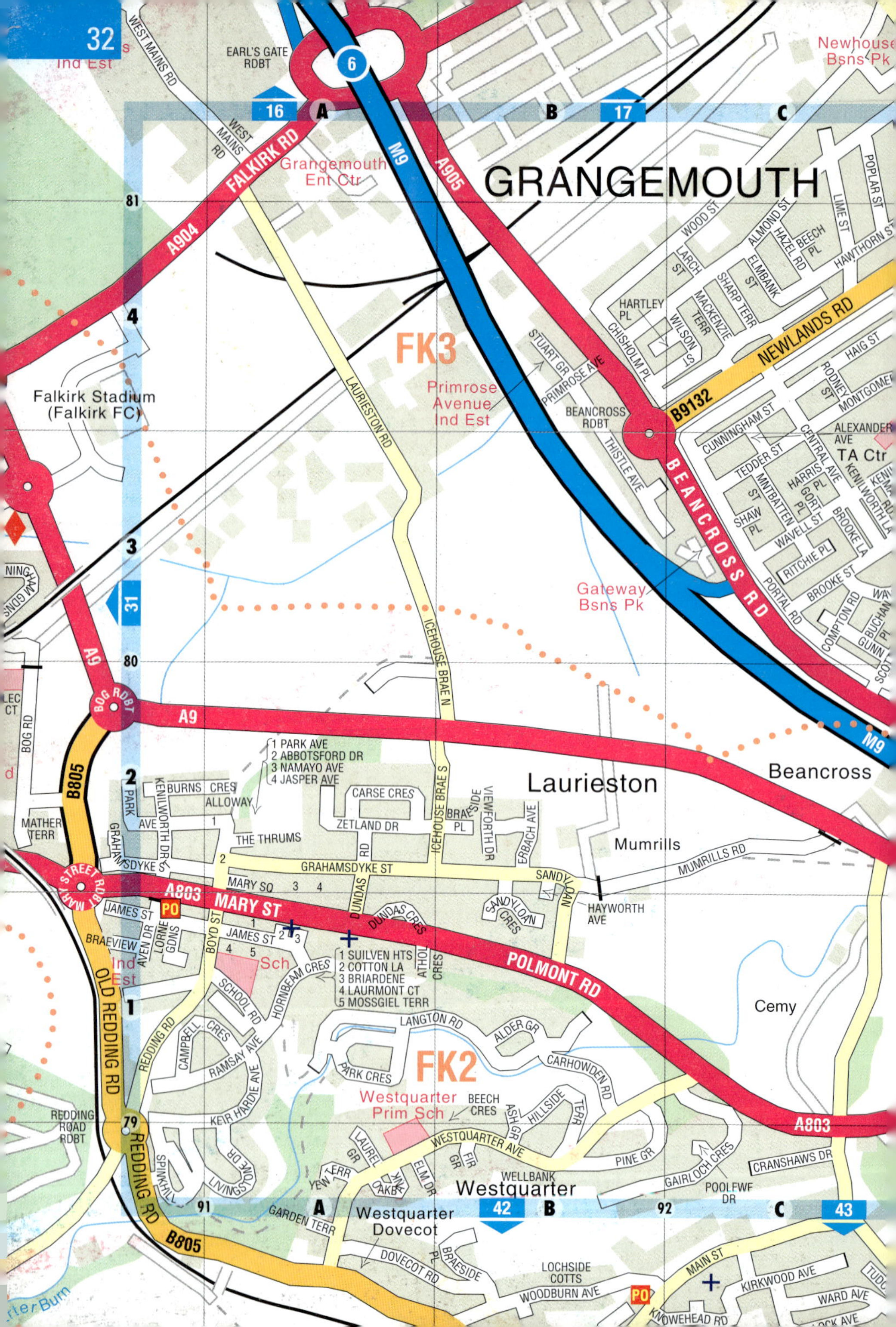

32
GRANGEMOUTH
Laurieston
Westquarter
Beancross
Mumrills
FK3
FK2
Earl's Gate Rdbt
Grangemouth Ent Ctr
Newhouse Bsns Pk
Falkirk Stadium (Falkirk FC)
Primrose Avenue Ind Est
Gateway Bsns Pk
Beancross Rdbt
Bog Rdbt
Mary Street Rdbt
Redding Road Rdbt
Westquarter Prim Sch
Westquarter Dovecot
TA Ctr
Cemy
Sch
Ind Est
PO
16
17
31
42
43
A
B
C
81
80
79
91
92
1
2
3
4
6
M9
A9
A904
A905
A803
B805
B9132
Falkirk Rd
West Mains Rd
Newlands Rd
Beancross Rd
Laurieston Rd
Icehouse Brae N
Icehouse Brae S
Mary St
Polmont Rd
Grahamsdyke St
Mumrills Rd
Old Redding Rd
Redding Rd
Bog Rd
Mather Terr
1 Park Ave
2 Abbotsford Dr
3 Namayo Ave
4 Jasper Ave
1 Suilven Hts
2 Cotton La
3 Briardene
4 Laurmont Ct
5 Mossgiel Terr
Burns Cres
Alloway
The Thrums
Carse Cres
Zetland Dr
Braeside Pl
Viewforth Dr
Erbach Ave
Sandyloan
Sandyloan Cres
Hayworth Ave
Dundas Rd
Dundas Cres
Athol Cres
Mary Sq
James St
Braeview
Aven Dr
Lorne Gdns
Boyd St
Hornbeam Cres
School Rd
Campbell Cres
Ramsay Ave
Keir Hardie Ave
Livingstone Dr
Spinkhill
Langton Rd
Alder Gr
Park Cres
Carhowden Rd
Hillside Terr
Ash Gr
Beech Cres
Westquarter Ave
Pine Gr
Gairloch Cres
Cranshaws Dr
Poolfwe Dr
Wellbank
Laurel Gr
Elm Dr
Fir Gr
Yew Terr
Garden Terr
Dovecot Rd
Braeside
Lochside Cotts
Woodburn Ave
Main St
Kirkwood Ave
Ward Ave
Knowehead Rd
Kenilworth Dr
Park Ave
Grahamsdyke St
Primrose Ave
Stuart Gr
Thistle Ave
Chisholm Pl
Wilson St
Hartley Pl
Mackenzie Terr
Sharp Terr
Larch St
Wood St
Elmbank St
Almond St
Hazel Rd
Beech Pl
Lime St
Poplar St
Hawthorn St
Haig St
Rodney St
Cunningham St
Central Ave
Alexander Ave
Tedder St
Harris Pl
Gort Pl
Mntbatten
Shaw Pl
Wavell St
Brooke La
Ritchie Pl
Brooke St
Portal Rd
Compton Rd
Buchan Pl
Gunn
Kenilworth

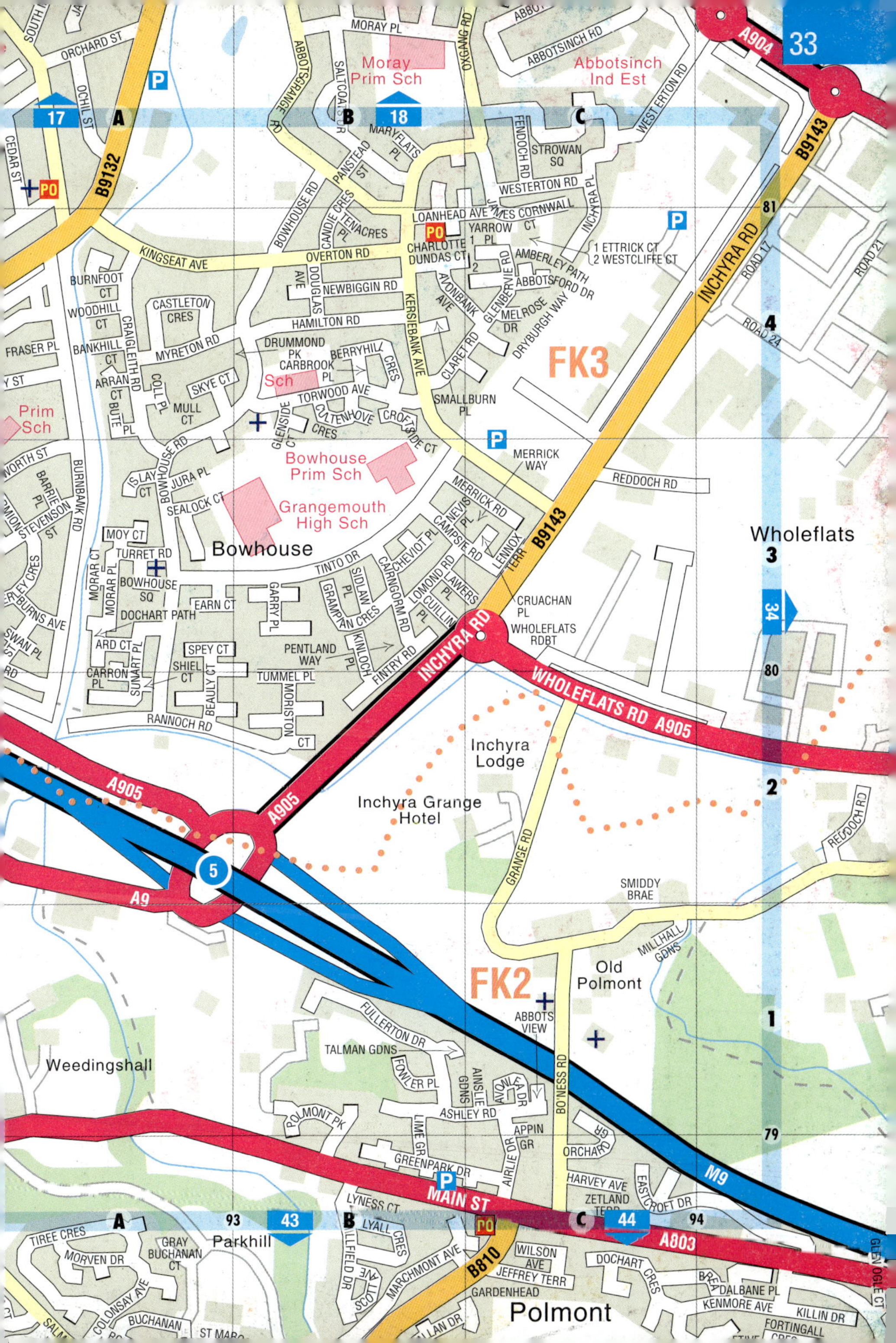
Moray Prim Sch
Abbotsinch Ind Est
FK3
Wholeflats
Bowhouse
Bowhouse Prim Sch
Grangemouth High Sch
Inchyra Lodge
Inchyra Grange Hotel
FK2
Old Polmont
Weedingshall
Parkhill
Polmont
INCHYRA RD
WHOLEFLATS RD A905
WHOLEFLATS RDBT
KINGSEAT AVE
OVERTON RD
MAIN ST
M9
A9
A905
A904
A803
B9143
B9132
B810
GRANGE RD
BO'NESS RD
REDDOCH RD
17
18
34
43
44
81
80
79
94
93
5

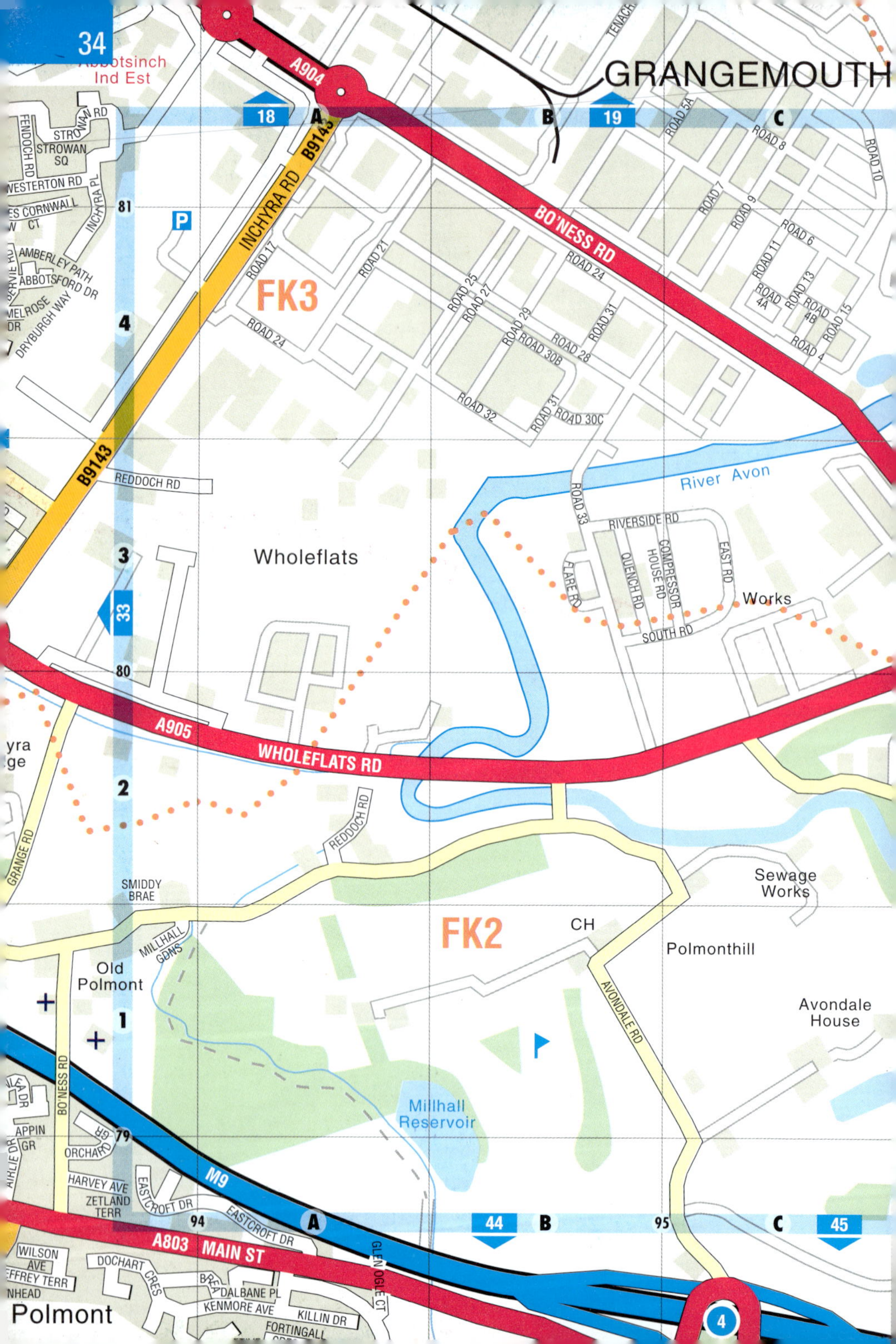

Abbotsinch Ind Est
GRANGEMOUTH
A904
18
19
A
B
C
B9143
STROWAN RD
STROWAN SQ
FENDOCH RD
WESTERTON RD
CORNWALL CT
INCHYRA PL
AMBERLEY PATH
ABBOTSFORD DR
MELROSE DR
DRYBURGH WAY
INCHYRA RD
81
4
FK3
ROAD 17
ROAD 21
ROAD 24
ROAD 25
ROAD 27
ROAD 29
ROAD 30B
ROAD 28
ROAD 31
ROAD 32
ROAD 30C
BO'NESS RD
ROAD 5A
ROAD 8
ROAD 10
ROAD 7
ROAD 9
ROAD 6
ROAD 11
ROAD 13
ROAD 4A
ROAD 4B
ROAD 15
ROAD 4
REDDOCH RD
River Avon
ROAD 33
RIVERSIDE RD
QUENCH RD
COMPRESSOR HOUSE RD
EAST RD
FLARE RD
SOUTH RD
Works
Wholeflats
3
33
80
A905
WHOLEFLATS RD
2
GRANGE RD
REDDOCH RD
SMIDDY BRAE
MILLHALL GDNS
FK2
CH
Polmonthill
Sewage Works
Old Polmont
1
AVONDALE RD
Avondale House
Millhall Reservoir
BO'NESS RD
APPIN GR
AIRLIE DR
ORCHARD GR
79
HARVEY AVE
ZETLAND TERR
EASTCROFT DR
M9
94
95
44
45
A803 MAIN ST
GLEN OGLE CT
WILSON AVE
JEFFREY TERR
DOCHART CRES
BREA
DALBANE PL
KENMORE AVE
KILLIN DR
FORTINGALL
Polmont
4

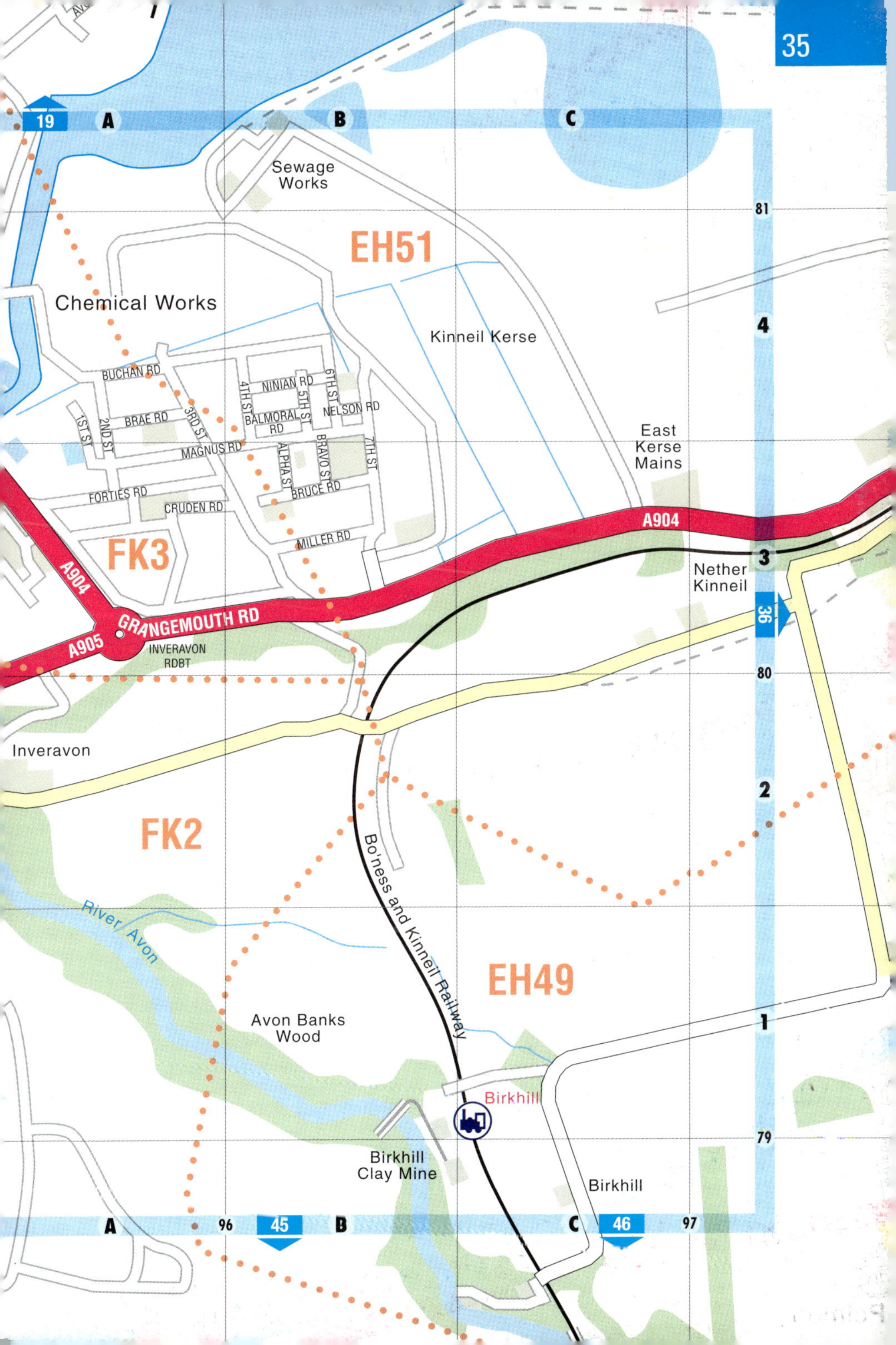
19
A
B
C
Sewage
Works
EH51
Chemical Works
Kinneil Kerse
BUCHAN RD
NINIAN RD
6TH ST
4TH ST
5TH ST
NELSON RD
1ST ST
2ND ST
BRAE RD
3RD ST
BALMORAL RD
MAGNUS RD
ALPHA ST
BRAVO ST
7TH ST
East
Kerse
Mains
FORTIES RD
CRUDEN RD
BRUCE RD
A904
MILLER RD
FK3
A904
Nether
Kinneil
GRANGEMOUTH RD
A905
INVERAVON
RDBT
36
Inveravon
FK2
Bo'ness and Kinneil Railway
River Avon
EH49
Avon Banks
Wood
Birkhill
Birkhill
Clay Mine
Birkhill
81
4
3
80
2
1
79
A
96
45
B
C
46
97

A
B
C
20
Slag Hill
Bo'ness & Kinneil
81
A904
4
EH51
GRANGEMOUTH RD
Kinneil Mus
& Roman Fortle
DUCHESS
ANNE
COTTS
Kinneil
House
PROVOST
CHESTNUT G
SYLVAN GR
East
Kerse
Mains
A904
3
Nether
Kinneil
Kinneil
Wood
35
80
2
Woodhead
Farm
Upper
Kinneil
1
EH49
Rousland
79
Birkhill
97
A
46
B
98
C
47

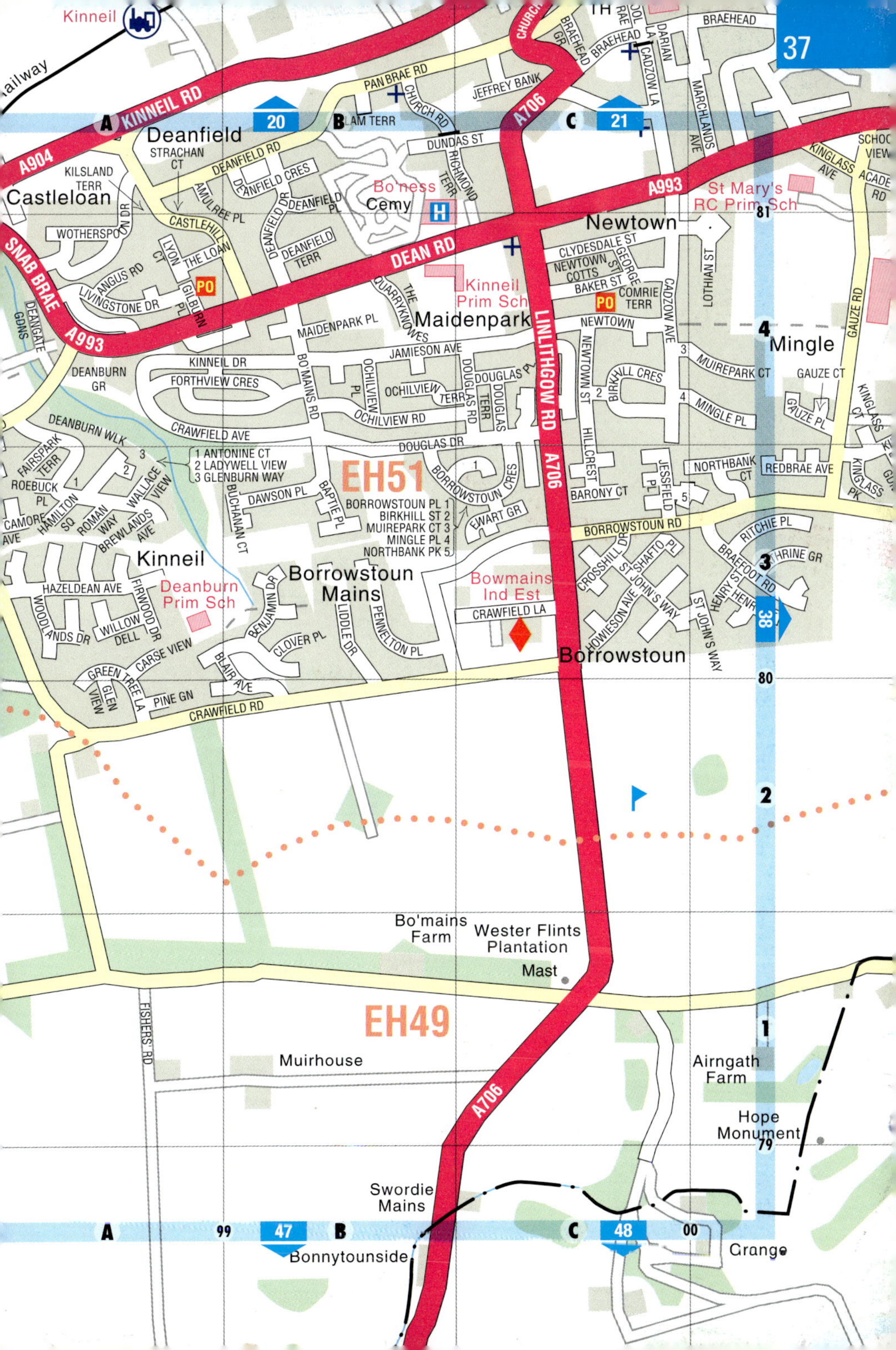

Kinneil
Railway
KINNEIL RD
A904
20
21
Deanfield
Castleloan
PAN BRAE RD
JEFFREY BANK
CHURCH RD
LAM TERR
DUNDAS ST
RICHMOND TERR
A706
BRAEHEAD
CADZOW LA
MARCHLANDS AVE
A993
KINGLASS AVE
ACADEMY RD
St Mary's RC Prim Sch
Bo'ness Cemy
Newtown
DEAN RD
SNAB BRAE
Kinneil Prim Sch
Maidenpark
LINLITHGOW RD
Mingle
GAUZE RD
GAUZE CT
MUIREPARK CT
MINGLE PL
BIRKHILL CRES
NEWTOWN ST
HILLCREST
BARONY CT
JESSFIELD PL
NORTHBANK CT
REDBRAE AVE
EH51
1 ANTONINE CT
2 LADYWELL VIEW
3 GLENBURN WAY
BORROWSTOUN PL 1
BIRKHILL ST 2
MUIREPARK CT 3
MINGLE PL 4
NORTHBANK PK 5
Kinneil
Borrowstoun Mains
Deanburn Prim Sch
Bowmains Ind Est
CRAWFIELD LA
Borrowstoun
BORROWSTOUN RD
CRAWFIELD RD
38
Bo'mains Farm
Wester Flints Plantation
Mast
EH49
Muirhouse
Airngath Farm
Hope Monument
Swordie Mains
47
48
Bonnytounside
Grange

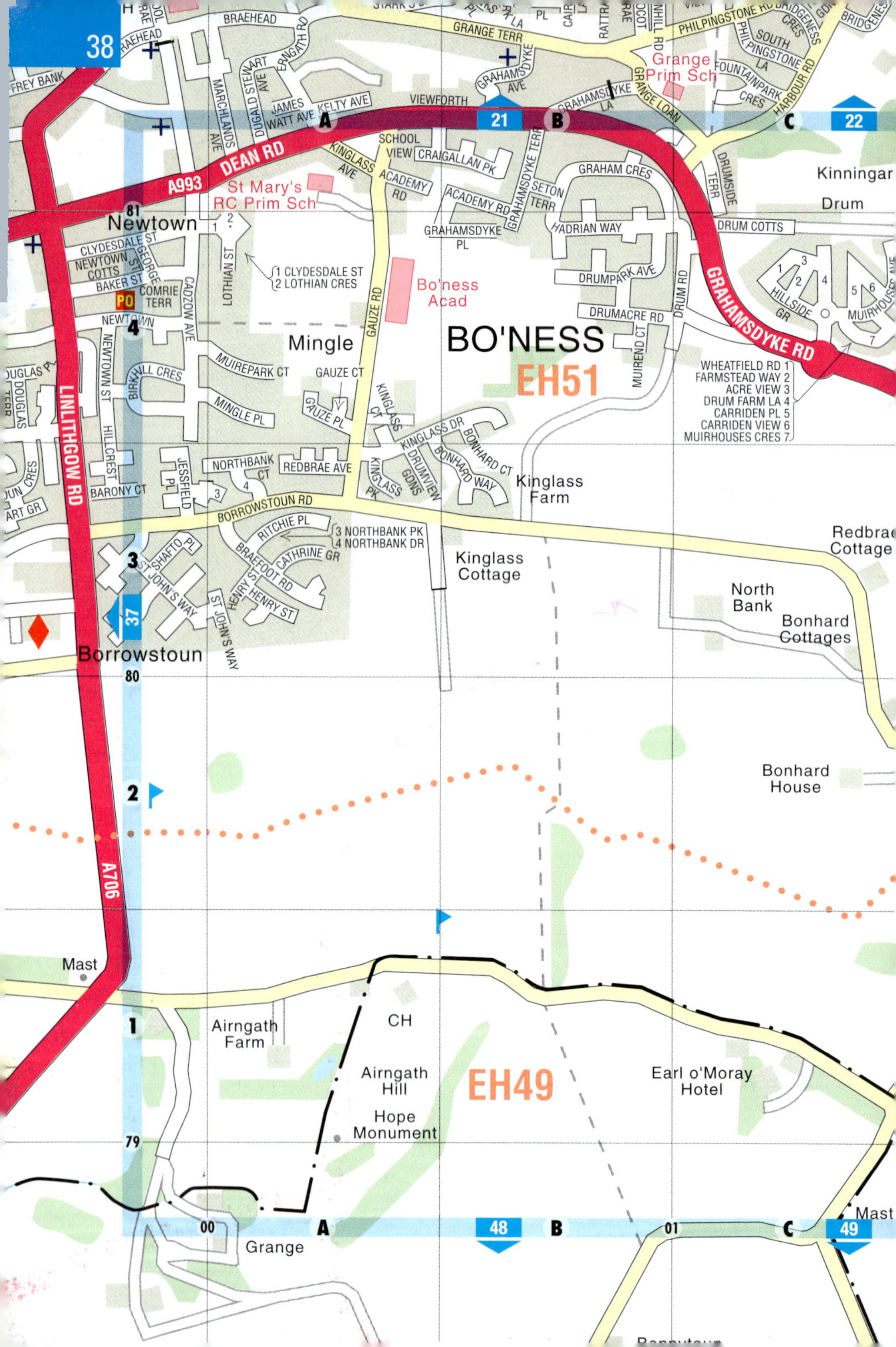

BO'NESS
EH51
EH49
Newtown
Mingle
Borrowstoun
Kinningar
Drum
Kinglass Farm
Kinglass Cottage
Redbrae Cottage
North Bank
Bonhard Cottages
Bonhard House
Mast
Airngath Farm
CH
Airngath Hill
Hope Monument
Earl o'Moray Hotel
Grange
St Mary's RC Prim Sch
Bo'ness Acad
Grange Prim Sch
DEAN RD
A993
GRAHAMSDYKE RD
LINLITHGOW RD
A706
BORROWSTOUN RD
GAUZE RD
GRANGE TERR
PHILPINGSTONE RD
BRIDGENESS CRES
SOUTH PHILPINGSTONE LA
FOUNTAINPARK CRES
HARBOUR RD
GRANGE LOAN
GRAHAMSDYKE LA
GRAHAMSDYKE AVE
VIEWFORTH
KELTY AVE
JAMES WATT AVE
DUGALD STEWART AVE
ERNGATH RD
BRAEHEAD
MARCHLANDS AVE
KINGLASS AVE
SCHOOL VIEW
CRAIGALLAN PK
ACADEMY RD
GRAHAMSDYKE TERR
SETON TERR
GRAHAM CRES
DRUMSIDE TERR
DRUM COTTS
HADRIAN WAY
DRUMPARK AVE
DRUM RD
DRUMACRE RD
MUIREND CT
HILLSIDE GR
MUIRHOUSES AVE
WHEATFIELD RD 1
FARMSTEAD WAY 2
ACRE VIEW 3
DRUM FARM LA 4
CARRIDEN PL 5
CARRIDEN VIEW 6
MUIRHOUSES CRES 7
GRAHAMSDYKE PL
CLYDESDALE ST
NEWTOWN COTTS
GEORGE ST
BAKER ST
COMRIE TERR
PO
NEWTOWN
LOTHIAN ST
1 CLYDESDALE ST
2 LOTHIAN CRES
CADZOW AVE
NEWTOWN ST
BIRKHILL CRES
MUIREPARK CT
MINGLE PL
GAUZE CT
KINGLASS CT
KINGLASS DR
BONHARD CT
BONHARD WAY
DRUMVIEW GDNS
KINGLASS PK
REDBRAE AVE
NORTHBANK CT
JESSFIELD PL
HILLCREST
BARONY CT
DOUGLAS
RITCHIE PL
3 NORTHBANK PK
4 NORTHBANK DR
CATHRINE GR
BRAFFOOT RD
HENRY ST
SHAFTO PL
ST JOHN'S WAY
A B C
21 22 37 48 49
81 80 79 00 01
4 3 2 1

Carriden Ind Est
CARRIDEN GLADE
KINACRES GR
FOREDALE TERR
Carriden
Park
22
Old Manse Wood
Firth of Forth
A904
The Old Manse
Cat Craig
Carriden Burn
MUIRHOUSES SQ
CARRIDEN BRAE
Carriden House
Carras Gate
ACRE RD
GLENARD VIEW
EH51
LITTLE CARRIDEN
HOPE COTTS
GLEDHILL AVE
MILLER CRES
Muirhouses
A993
Willie White's Clump
Wester Bonhard
Bonhard Place
Bonhard Old Mill
East Bonhard Farm
EH49
Walton
Dyland Cottages
Woolstoun
B903
WOODLEA COTTS
Champany Inn
Grougfoot Farm
A803
49
A
B
C
02
03
79
80
81
1
2
3
4

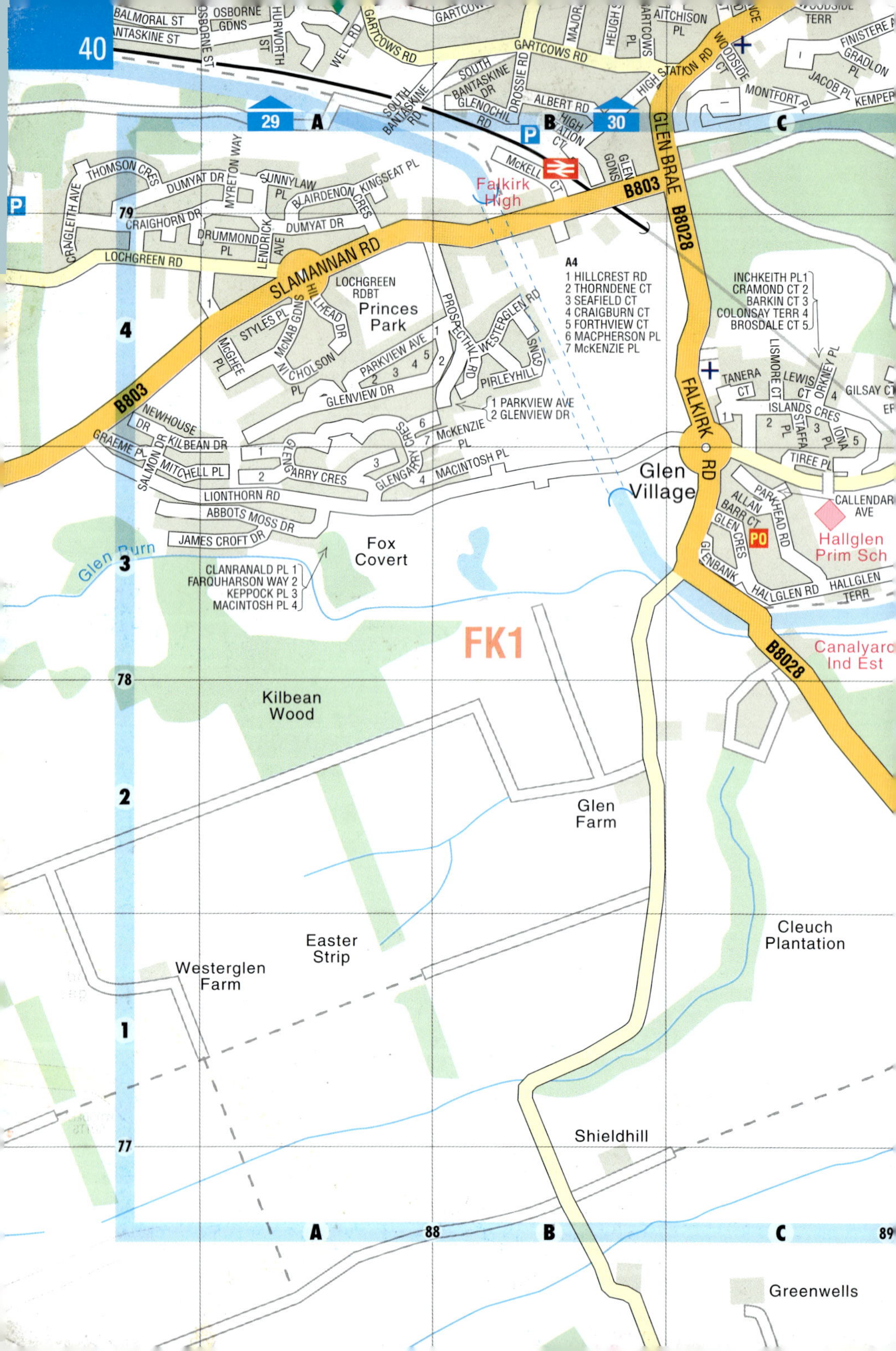

29
30
A
B
C
Falkirk High
Princes Park
LOCHGREEN RDBT
A4
1 HILLCREST RD
2 THORNDENE CT
3 SEAFIELD CT
4 CRAIGBURN CT
5 FORTHVIEW CT
6 MACPHERSON PL
7 McKENZIE PL
INCHKEITH PL 1
CRAMOND CT 2
BARKIN CT 3
COLONSAY TERR 4
BROSDALE CT 5
1 PARKVIEW AVE
2 GLENVIEW DR
CLANRANALD PL 1
FARQUHARSON WAY 2
KEPPOCK PL 3
MACINTOSH PL 4
SLAMANNAN RD
B803
B8028
GLEN BRAE
FALKIRK RD
LOCHGREEN RD
LIONTHORN RD
ABBOTS MOSS DR
JAMES CROFT DR
Glen Village
Fox Covert
Glen Burn
Hallglen Prim Sch
Canalyard Ind Est
FK1
Kilbean Wood
Glen Farm
Easter Strip
Westerglen Farm
Cleuch Plantation
Shieldhill
Greenwells
79
78
77
88
89
4
3
2
1

Callendar House
Callendar Park
Callendar Wood
Mausoleum
Woodend Farm
Hallglen
Westquarter Burn
Union Canal
FK1
FK2
Mavisbank
Mavisbank Wood
Easter Pirleyhill
Wester Pirleyhill
Pirleyhill Bridge
Easter Shieldhill
Shieldhill
NEW HALLGLEN RD
GLENBURN RD
REDDING ROAD RDBT
B805
B8028
B810
CROSS BRAE
MAIN ST
CALIFORNIA RD
CALLENDAR BVD
30
31
42
50

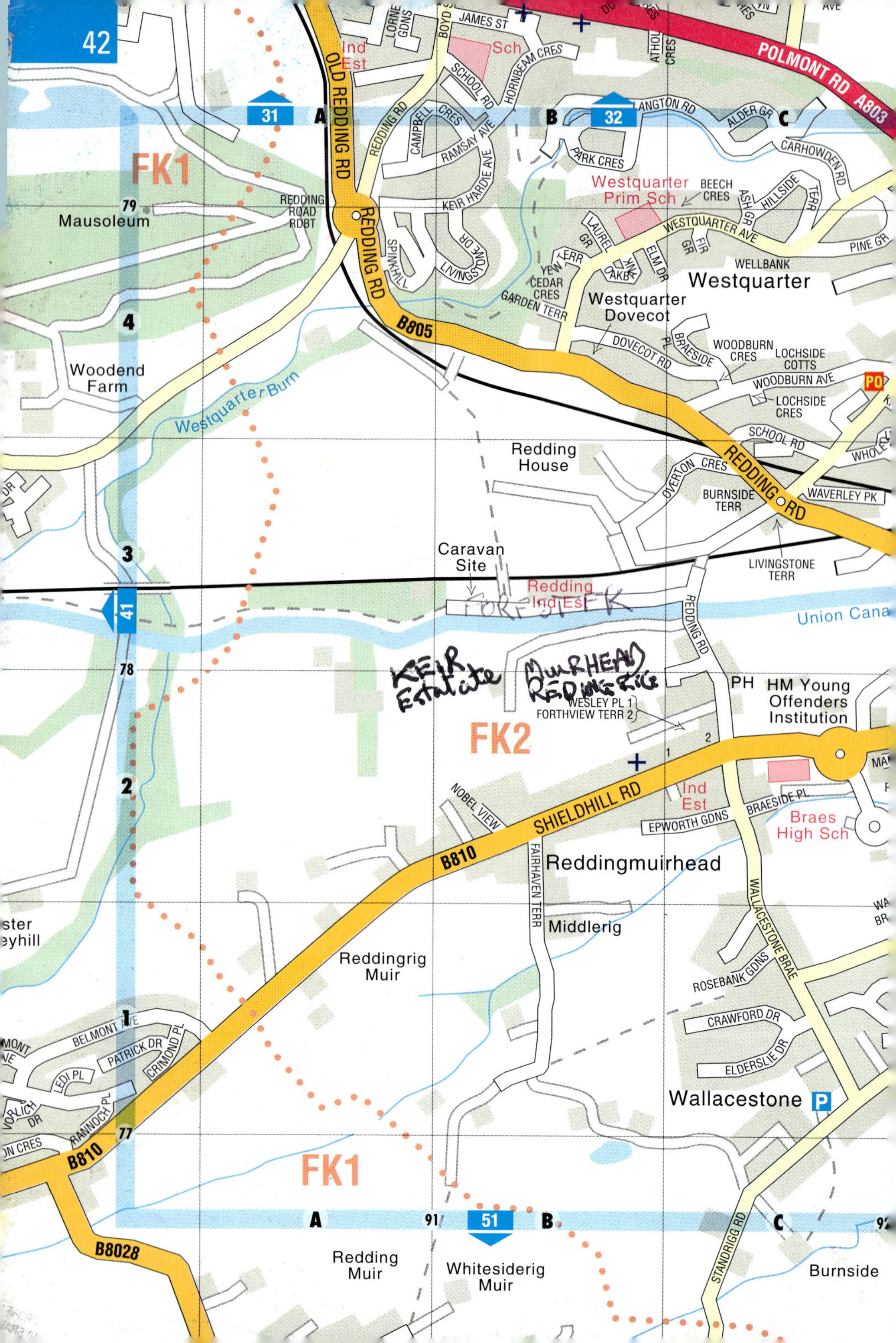
31
32
41
51
A
B
C
FK1
FK2
79
78
77
91
4
3
2
1
OLD REDDING RD
REDDING RD
JAMES ST
LORNE GDNS
BOYD ST
Ind Est
Sch
SCHOOL RD
HORNBEAM CRES
ATHOLL CRES
POLMONT RD A803
LANGTON RD
ALDER GR
CARHOWDEN RD
CAMPBELL CRES
RAMSAY AVE
KEIR HARDIE AVE
PARK CRES
Westquarter Prim Sch
BEECH CRES
ASH GR
HILLSIDE TERR
WESTQUARTER AVE
PINE GR
LAUREL GR
ELM DR
FIR GR
OAK BANK
YEW TERR
CEDAR CRES
GARDEN TERR
WELLBANK
Westquarter
Westquarter Dovecot
SPINKHILL
LIVINGSTONE DR
Mausoleum
REDDING ROAD RDBT
Woodend Farm
Westquarter Burn
B805
DOVECOT RD
BRAESIDE PL
WOODBURN CRES
LOCHSIDE COTTS
WOODBURN AVE
LOCHSIDE CRES
PO
SCHOOL RD
WHOLE
Redding House
OVERTON CRES
BURNSIDE TERR
WAVERLEY PK
LIVINGSTONE TERR
Caravan Site
Redding Ind Est
Union Canal
PH
HM Young Offenders Institution
WESLEY PL 1
FORTHVIEW TERR 2
Ind Est
BRAESIDE PL
Braes High Sch
EPWORTH GDNS
NOBEL VIEW
SHIELDHILL RD
B810
FAIRHAVEN TERR
Reddingmuirhead
Middlerig
WALLACESTONE BRAE
Reddingrig Muir
ROSEBANK GDNS
CRAWFORD DR
ELDERSLIE DR
Wallacestone
P
BELMONT AVE
PATRICK DR
CRIMOND PL
LEDI PL
RANNOCH PL
VORLICH DR
B8028
Redding Muir
Whitesiderig Muir
STANDRIGG RD
Burnside
MAR

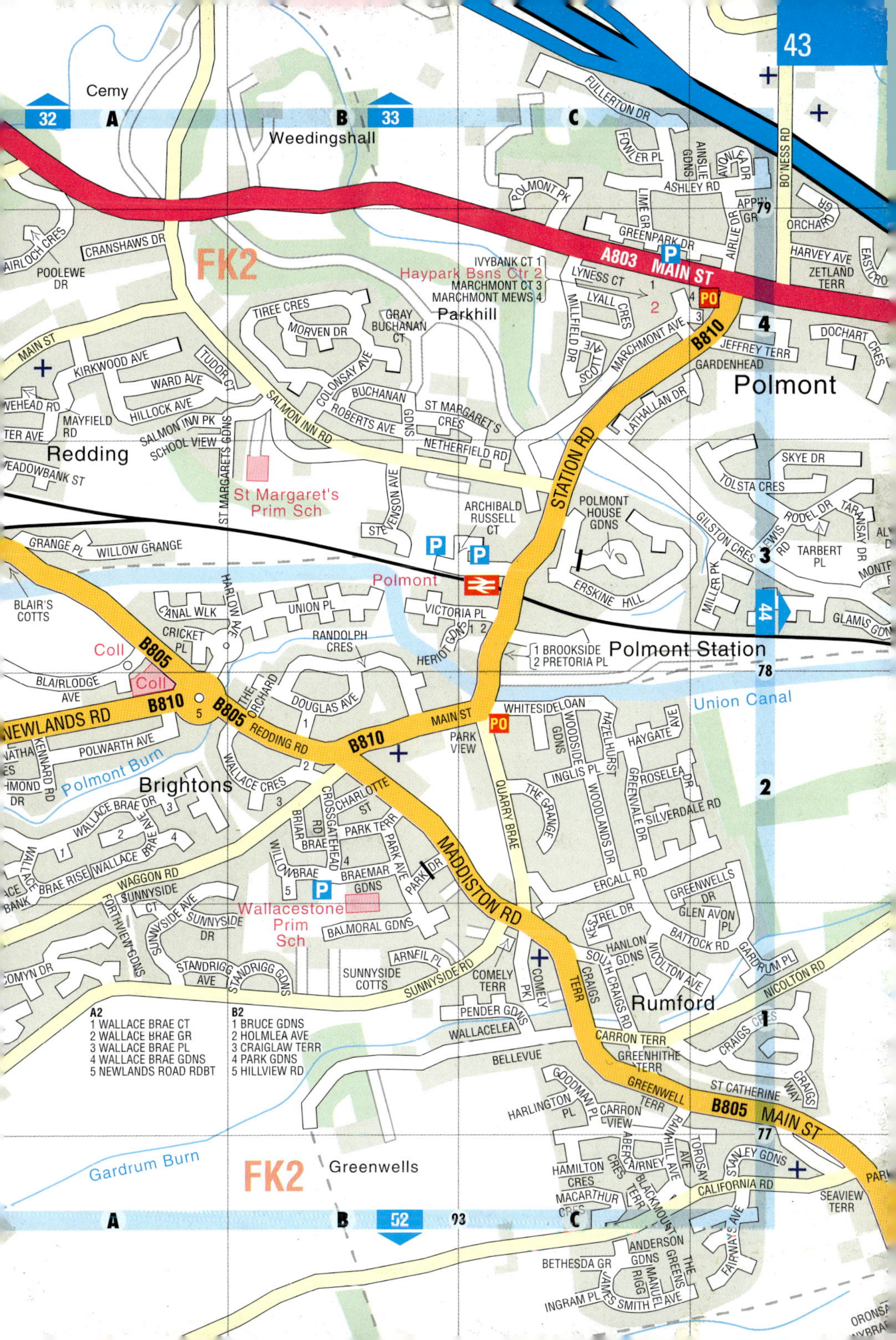

43
32
33
44
52
A
B
C
1
2
3
4
79
78
77
93
Cemy
Weedingshall
FK2
Parkhill
Polmont
Redding
Polmont Station
Brightons
Rumford
Greenwells
Union Canal
Polmont Burn
Gardrum Burn
A803 MAIN ST
B810
B805
STATION RD
NEWLANDS RD
REDDING RD
MADDISTON RD
MAIN ST
FULLERTON DR
FOWLER PL
POLMONT PK
AINSLIE GDNS
AVONLEA DR
ASHLEY RD
LIME GR
GREENPARK DR
AIRLIE DR
BO'NESS RD
ORCHARD GR
HARVEY AVE
ZETLAND TERR
LYNESS CT
LYALL CRES
MILLFIELD DR
SCOTT AVE
MARCHMONT AVE
JEFFREY TERR
GARDENHEAD
DOCHART CRES
IVYBANK CT 1
Haypark Bsns Ctr 2
MARCHMONT CT 3
MARCHMONT MEWS 4
CRANSHAWS DR
FAIRLOCH CRES
POOLEWE DR
TIREE CRES
MORVEN DR
GRAY BUCHANAN CT
COLONSAY AVE
BUCHANAN GDNS
ROBERTS AVE
ST MARGARET'S CRES
NETHERFIELD RD
SALMON INN RD
KIRKWOOD AVE
TUDOR CT
WARD AVE
HILLOCK AVE
MAYFIELD RD
SALMON INN PK
SCHOOL VIEW
ST MARGARETS GDNS
St Margaret's Prim Sch
LATHALLAN DR
SKYE DR
TOLSTA CRES
RODEL DR
TARANSAY DR
TARBERT PL
LEWIS RD
GILSTON CRES
MILLER PK
GLAMIS GDNS
STEVENSON AVE
ARCHIBALD RUSSELL CT
POLMONT HOUSE GDNS
ERSKINE HILL
Polmont
GRANGE PL
WILLOW GRANGE
BLAIR'S COTTS
CANAL WLK
HARLOW AVE
UNION PL
VICTORIA PL
HERIOT GDNS
1 BROOKSIDE
2 PRETORIA PL
CRICKET PL
RANDOLPH CRES
Coll
BLAIRLODGE AVE
THE ORCHARD
DOUGLAS AVE
WHITESIDELOAN
WOODSIDE GDNS
HAZELHURST
HAYGATE AVE
PARK VIEW
KENNARD RD
POLWARTH AVE
INGLIS PL
ROSELEA DR
GREENVALE DR
SILVERDALE RD
WOODLANDS DR
QUARRY BRAE
THE GRANGE
WALLACE CRES
CHARLOTTE ST
CROSSGATEHEAD RD
BRIAR BRAE
PARK TERR
PARK AVE
PARK DR
WALLACE BRAE DR
WALLACE BRAE AVE
WALLACE BRAE RISE
WAGGON RD
SUNNYSIDE CT
SUNNYSIDE AVE
SUNNYSIDE DR
WILLOWBRAE
BRAEMAR GDNS
Wallacestone Prim Sch
BALMORAL GDNS
ERCALL RD
GREENWELLS DR
GLEN AVON PL
KESTREL DR
BATTOCK RD
HANLON GDNS
NICOLTON AVE
GARDRUM PL
NICOLTON RD
SOUTH CRAIGS RD
CRAIGS TERR
COMLEY PK
COMELY TERR
ARNEIL PL
SUNNYSIDE RD
SUNNYSIDE COTTS
FORTHVIEW GDNS
COMYN DR
STANDRIGG AVE
STANDRIGG GDNS
PENDER GDNS
WALLACELEA
BELLEVUE
CARRON TERR
GREENHITHE TERR
CRAIGS CRES
CRAIGS WAY
ST CATHERINE
GREENWELL TERR
GOODMAN PL
HARLINGTON PL
CARRON VIEW
RAINHILL AVE
TOROSAY
STANLEY GDNS
ABERCAIRNEY
BLACKMOUNT TERR
HAMILTON CRES
MACARTHUR CRES
CALIFORNIA RD
SEAVIEW TERR
FAIRWAYS AVE
ANDERSON GDNS
THE GREENS
MANUEL AVE
BETHESDA GR
JAMES SMITH
RIGG
INGRAM PL
A2
1 WALLACE BRAE CT
2 WALLACE BRAE GR
3 WALLACE BRAE PL
4 WALLACE BRAE GDNS
5 NEWLANDS ROAD RDBT
B2
1 BRUCE GDNS
2 HOLMLEA AVE
3 CRAIGLAW TERR
4 PARK GDNS
5 HILLVIEW RD

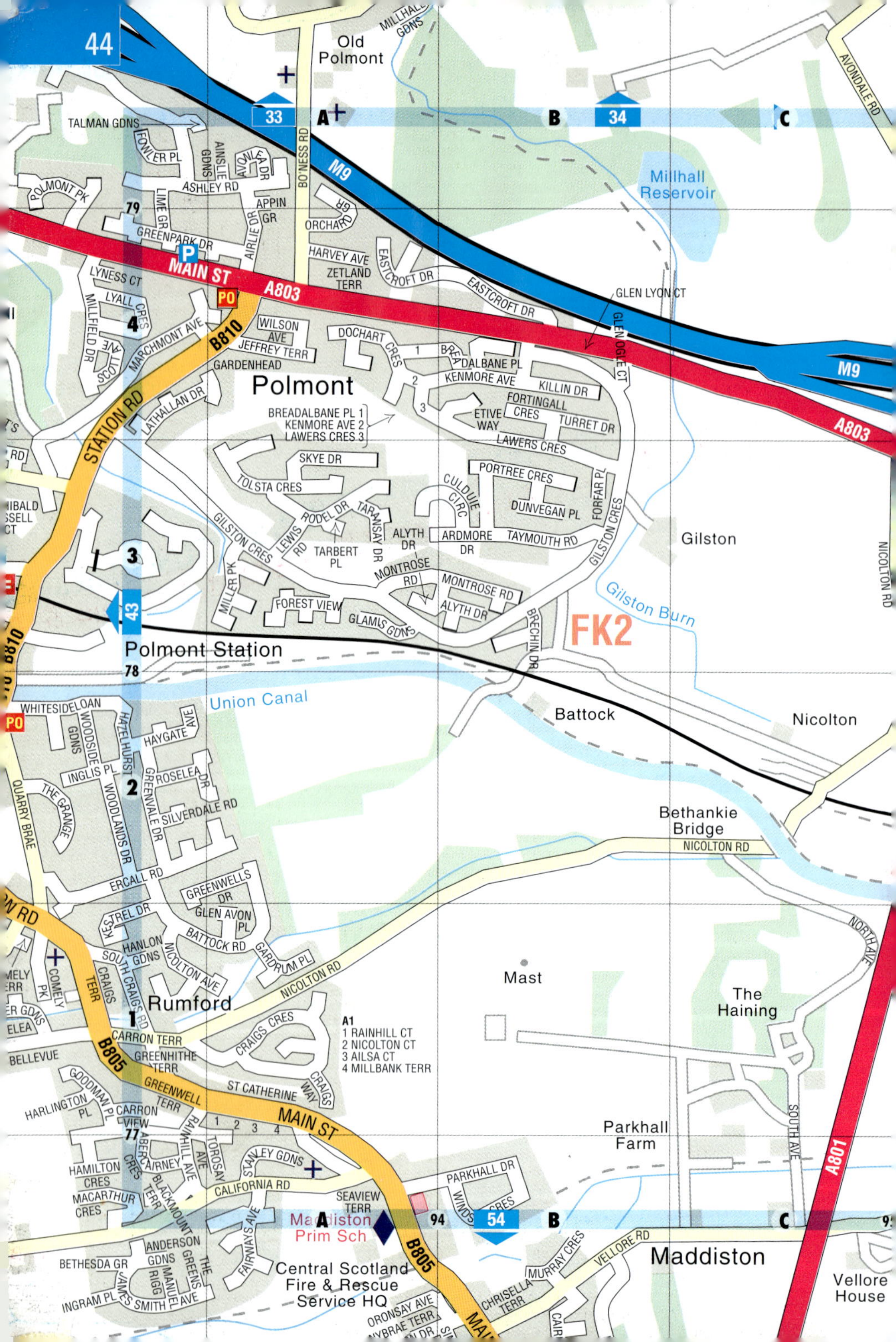

Old Polmont
MILLHALL GDNS
33
34
A
B
C
AVONDALE RD
TALMAN GDNS
FOWLER PL
AINSLIE GDNS
AVONLEA DR
BO'NESS RD
M9
Millhall Reservoir
POLMONT PK
ASHLEY RD
79
LIME GR
APPIN GR
AIRLIE DR
ORCHARD GR
GREENPARK DR
P
MAIN ST
HARVEY AVE
ZETLAND TERR
EASTCROFT DR
A803
LYNESS CT
LYALL CRES
PO
MILLFIELD DR
4
SCOTT AVE
MARCHMONT AVE
B810
WILSON AVE
JEFFREY TERR
GARDENHEAD
DOCHART CRES
BREA
DALBANE PL
KENMORE AVE
GLEN LYON CT
GLEN OGLE CT
KILLIN DR
Polmont
LATHALLAN DR
BREADALBANE PL 1
KENMORE AVE 2
LAWERS CRES 3
FORTINGALL CRES
ETIVE WAY
TURRET DR
LAWERS CRES
STATION RD
SKYE DR
TOLSTA CRES
PORTREE CRES
CULDUIE CIRC
FORFAR PL
DUNVEGAN PL
GILSTON CRES
RODEL DR
TARANSAY DR
LEWIS RD
TARBERT PL
ALYTH DR
ARDMORE DR
TAYMOUTH RD
Gilston
3
MONTROSE RD
MONTROSE RD
MILLER PK
FOREST VIEW
ALYTH DR
GLAMIS GDNS
43
BRECHIN DR
FK2
Gilston Burn
NICOLTON RD
Polmont Station
78
Union Canal
Battock
Nicolton
WHITESIDELOAN
WOODSIDE GDNS
HAZELHURST
HAYGATE AVE
INGLIS PL
ROSELEA DR
2
GREENVALE DR
THE GRANGE
WOODLANDS DR
QUARRY BRAE
SILVERDALE RD
Bethankie Bridge
NICOLTON RD
ERCALL RD
GREENWELLS DR
GLEN AVON PL
KESTREL DR
HANLON GDNS
BATTOCK RD
GARDRUM PL
NICOLTON AVE
SOUTH CRAIGS RD
CRAIGS TERR
COMELY PK
NORTH AVE
Mast
The Haining
Rumford
1
CRAIGS CRES
A1
1 RAINHILL CT
2 NICOLTON CT
3 AILSA CT
4 MILLBANK TERR
CARRON TERR
BELLEVUE
GREENHITHE TERR
B805
GOODMAN PL
HARLINGTON PL
ST CATHERINE
CRAIGS WAY
GREENWELL TERR
CARRON VIEW
MAIN ST
RAINHILL AVE
TOROSAY
1 2 3 4
77
ABERCAIRNEY CRES
STANLEY GDNS
Parkhall Farm
HAMILTON CRES
SOUTH AVE
PARKHALL DR
A801
BLACKMOUNT TERR
CALIFORNIA RD
MACARTHUR CRES
SEAVIEW TERR
WINDSOR CRES
FAIRWAYS AVE
Maddiston Prim Sch
94
54
ANDERSON GDNS
VELLORE RD
MURRAY CRES
Maddiston
BETHESDA GR
THE GREENS
MANUEL AVE
RIGG
JAMES SMITH
INGRAM PL
Central Scotland Fire & Rescue Service HQ
CHRISELLA TERR
ORONSAY AVE
Vellore House
NICOLTON RD

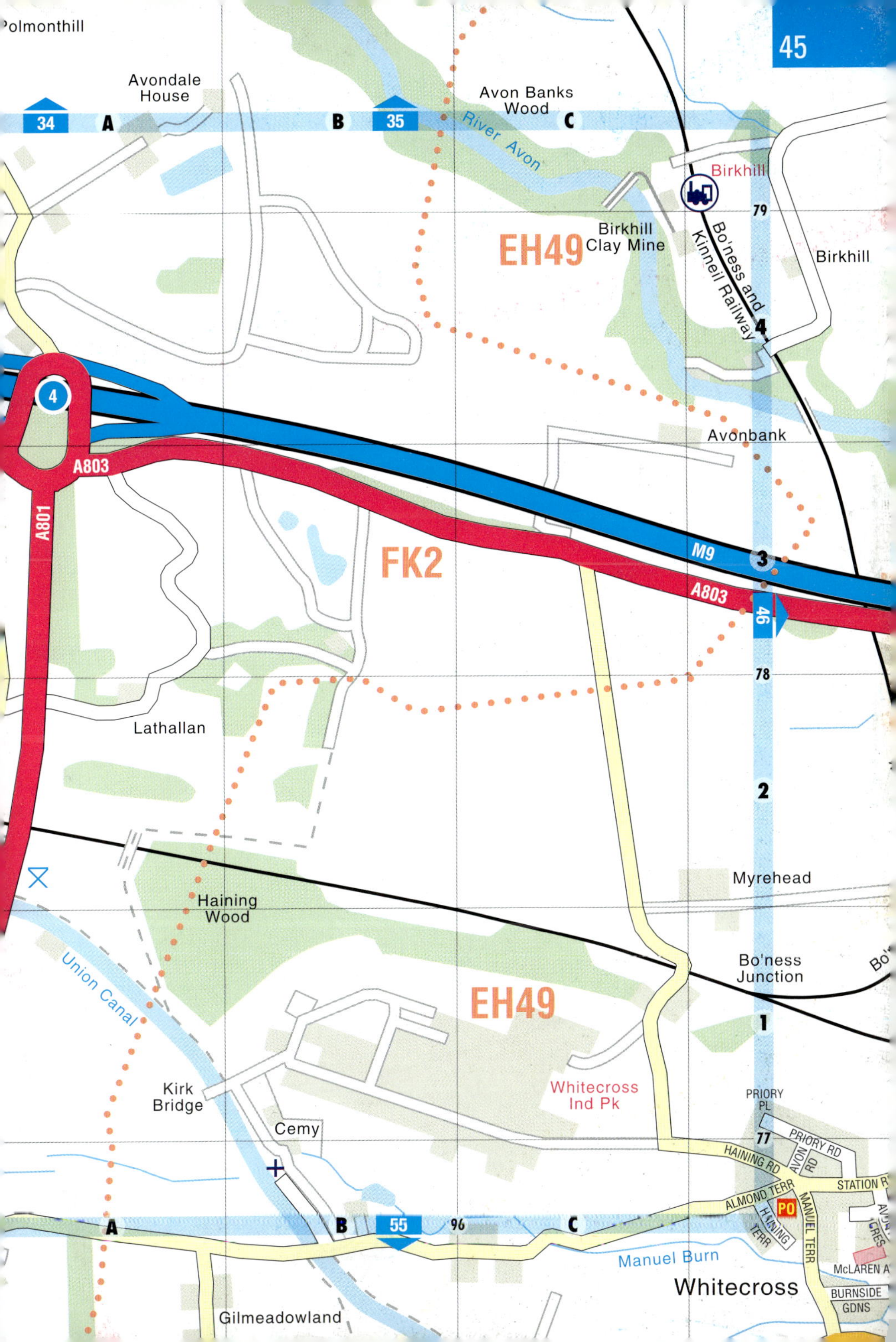
Polmonthill
Avondale House
34
A
B
35
C
Avon Banks Wood
River Avon
Birkhill
Birkhill Clay Mine
EH49
Bo'ness and Kinneil Railway
79
Birkhill
4
4
Avonbank
A803
A801
FK2
M9
3
A803
46
78
Lathallan
2
Myrehead
Haining Wood
Bo'ness Junction
Union Canal
EH49
1
Kirk Bridge
Whitecross Ind Pk
PRIORY PL
Cemy
77
PRIORY RD
HAINING RD
AVON RD
STATION RD
ALMOND TERR
PO
HAINING TERR
MANUEL TERR
A
B
55
96
C
Manuel Burn
McLAREN A
Whitecross
BURNSIDE GDNS
Gilmeadowland

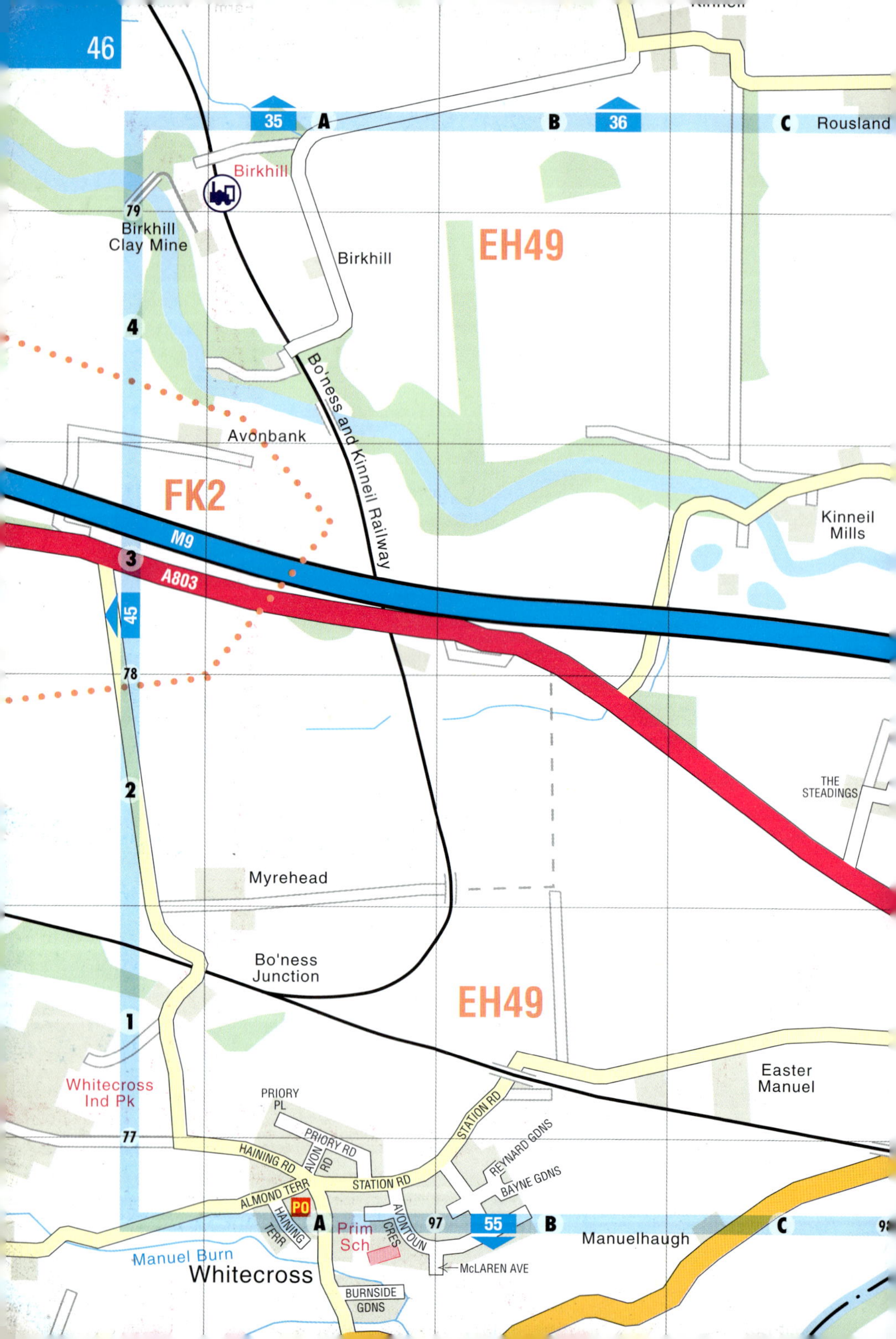
35
A
B
36
C
Rousland
Birkhill
79
Birkhill
Clay Mine
Birkhill
EH49
4
Bo'ness and Kinneil Railway
Avonbank
FK2
M9
Kinneil
Mills
3
A803
45
78
THE
STEADINGS
2
Myrehead
Bo'ness
Junction
EH49
1
Whitecross
Ind Pk
Easter
Manuel
PRIORY
PL
STATION RD
PRIORY RD
REYNARD GDNS
77
HAINING RD
AVON
RD
STATION RD
BAYNE GDNS
ALMOND TERR
PO
HAINING
TERR
A
Prim
Sch
CRES
AVONTOUN
97
55
B
Manuelhaugh
C
Manuel Burn
Whitecross
McLAREN AVE
BURNSIDE
GDNS

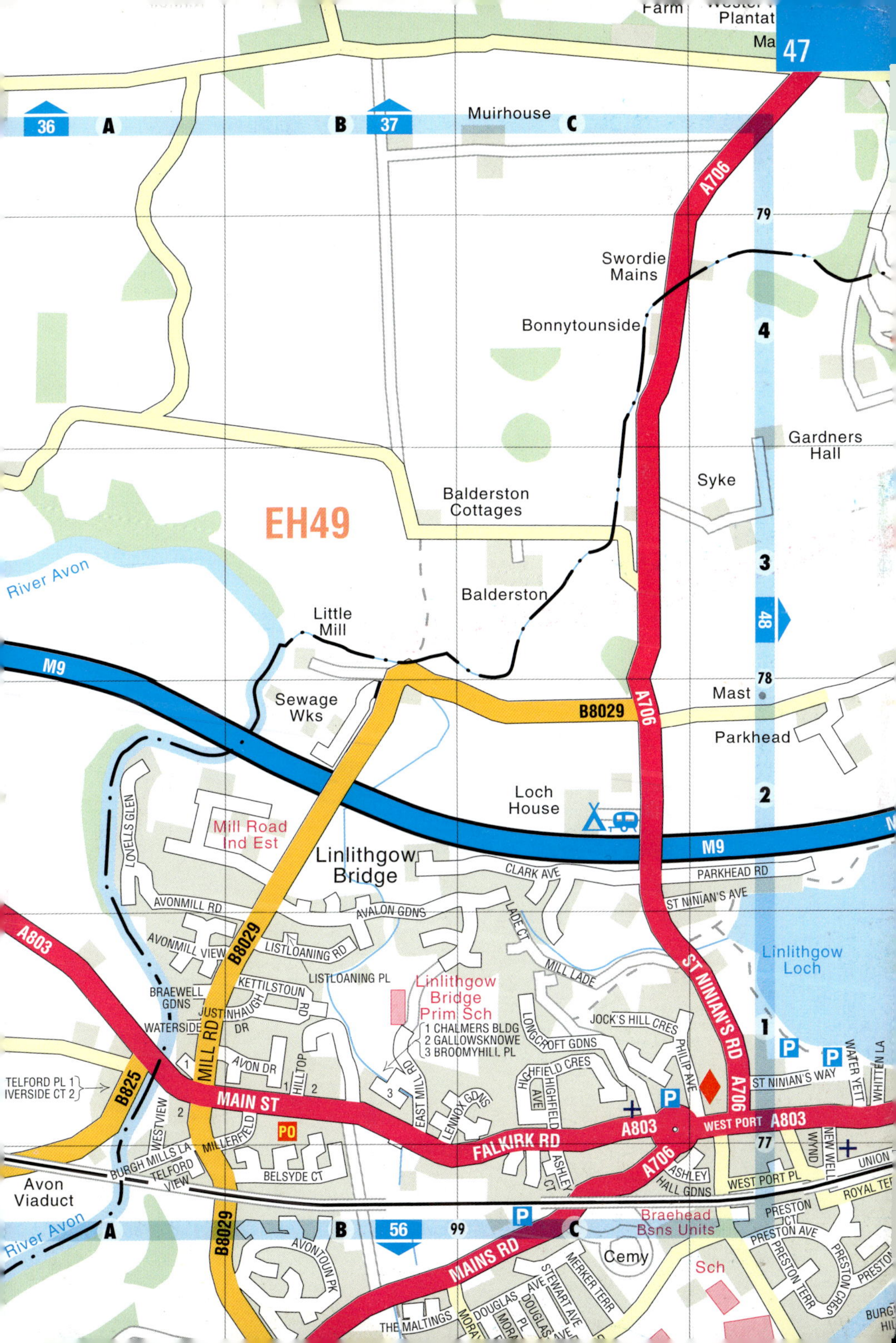
47
36
A
B
37
Muirhouse
C
A706
79
Swordie
Mains
Bonnytounside
4
Gardners
Hall
Syke
Balderston
Cottages
EH49
River Avon
3
48
Balderston
Little
Mill
M9
Sewage
Wks
78
Mast
B8029
Parkhead
Loch
House
2
Mill Road
Ind Est
Linlithgow
Bridge
CLARK AVE
PARKHEAD RD
ST NINIAN'S AVE
LOVELLS GLEN
AVONMILL RD
AVALON GDNS
LADE CT
A803
AVONMILL VIEW
LISTLOANING RD
B8029
MILL LADE
Linlithgow
Loch
ST NINIAN'S RD
LISTLOANING PL
Linlithgow
Bridge
Prim Sch
BRAEWELL
GDNS
KETTILSTOUN
RD
JUSTINHAUGH
DR
JOCK'S HILL CRES
1
WATERSIDE
1 CHALMERS BLDG
2 GALLOWSKNOWE
3 BROOMYHILL PL
LONGCROFT GDNS
PHILIP AVE
WATER YETT
WHITTEN LA
AVON DR
HILLTOP
MILL RD
HIGHFIELD CRES
TELFORD PL 1
IVERSIDE CT 2
B825
MAIN ST
EAST MILL RD
LENNOX GDNS
HIGHFIELD AVE
ST NINIAN'S WAY
WESTVIEW
PO
A803
WEST PORT
A803
FALKIRK RD
MILLERFIELD
A706
77
WYND
NEW WELL
BURGH MILLS LA
TELFORD VIEW
ASHLEY CT
ASHLEY HALL GDNS
UNION
WEST PORT PL
ROYAL TER
Avon
Viaduct
BELSYDE CT
Braehead
Bsns Units
PRESTON CT
PRESTON AVE
A
B
56
99
C
River Avon
B8029
AVONTOUN PK
MAINS RD
Cemy
Sch
PRESTON TERR
PRESTON CRES
DOUGLAS AVE
STEWART AVE
MERKER TERR
THE MALTINGS
MORAY
DOUGLAS PL
BURGH
Farm
Plantat

Plantation
Mast
Airngath Farm
CH
Airngath Hill
Hope Monument
37
A
B
38
C
A706
79
Swordie Mains
Bonnytounside
4
Grange
Bonnytoun Cottages
Gardners Hall
Syke
Bonnytoun Farm
EH49
3
47
PARKHEAD SMALLHOLDINGS
78
Mast
B8029
Parkhead
M9
Mount Michael
Loch House
2
M9
A803
CLARK AVE
PARKHEAD RD
Linlithgow Loch
Barons Hill
ST NINIAN'S AVE
1 DOG WELL WYND
2 THE CROSS
3 ST MICHAEL'S WYND
4 STATION RD
LADE CT
MILL LADE
ST NINIAN'S RD
Linlithgow Palace
Low Port Prim Sch
ST MICHAELS LA
BLACKNESS RD
BARONS HILL AVE
BARONS HILL CT
1 HAMILTON PK
2 ST JOHN'S AVE
3 LION WELL WYND
JOCK'S HILL CRES
LONGCROFT GDNS
PHILIP AVE
WATER YETT
WHITTEN LA
Liby
KIRKGATE
TH
MARKET LA
THE VENNEL
PROVOST RD
REGENT SQ
MADDERFIELD MEWS
HIGHFIELD CRES
HIGHFIELD AVE
ST NINIAN'S WAY
Mus
HIGH ST
HIGH PORT
A706
PO
B9080
EDINB
A803
WEST PORT
HIGH ST
A803
Ct
BACK STATION RD
ST MAGDALENE
Linlithgow
ALKIRK RD
77
A706
ASHLEY CT
WYND
NEW WELL
UNION RD
STRAWBERRY BANK
MANSE RD
ASHLEY HALL GDNS
WEST PORT PL
ROYAL TERR
AVON PL
CANAL TERR
Braehead Bsns Units
PRESTON RD
PRESTON CT
BARKHILL RD
Linlithgow Canal Ctr
ROCKVILLE GR
CLARENDON CRES
A
00
57
B
C
S RD
Cemy
Sch
PRESTON TERR
PRESTON CRES
PRESTON PK
FRIARS BRAE
CLARENDON RD
LIN
MERKER TERR
STEWART AVE
DOUGLAS AVE
BURGESS HILL
FRIARS LOAN
Friar's
Clarendon House

38
A
B
39
C
o' Moray
Hotel
Woolstoun
B903
79
Champany Inn
A904 Forth Road Bridge (A90)
Grougfoot
Farm
A803
4
Mast
M9 Edinburgh (M8), Forth Road Bridge (A90)
3
Burgh Muir
Works
EH49
Burghmuir
78
A803
Burgh
Muir
GRANGE KNOWE
PILGRIMS HILL
BURGHMUIR CT
GRANGE VIEW
2
BONNYTOUN TERR
BONNYTOUN AVE
Springfield
Prim Sch
KINGSFIELD
SHERIFFS PK
DOVECOT PK
SPRINGFIELD CT
SPRINGFIELD RD
HUNTBURN AVE
BELLS BURN AVE
CARSE KNOWE
BAILIELANDS
1
Wilcoxholm
Towing Path
MAIDLANDS
HILLSIDE
COTTS
GH RD
Union Canal
Pilgrim's
Hill
77
Cemy
St Michael's
A
B
02
C
ITHGOW
B9080
Porterside

Pirleyhill
Wester Pirleyhill
Westquarter Burn
A
41
B
C
Pirleyhill Bridge
B8028
BELMONT AVE
BELMONT AVE
PATRICK DR
CRIMOND PL
EASTON DR
OCHIL VIEW
LEDI PL
WALLACE VIEW
GARDRUM GDNS
BRAES VIEW
VORLICH DR
RANNOCH PL
PATERSON DR
77
HIGH VIEW GR
CROSS BRAE
CRUICKSHANK DR
PIRLEYHILL DR
ANDERSON CRES
B810
PARK END CT
HEATHER AVE
HERDSHILL AVE
ROSEMOUNT GDNS
MUIRPARK DR
PO
MAIN ST
B8028
MAVISBANK AVE
GREENCRAIG AVE
GREENMOUNT DR
BRAESIDE
Easter Shieldhill
4
CROSSHALL PL
CALIFORNIA RD
Greenwells
Shieldhill
ELIM DR
Shieldhill Prim Sch
Burnside
Polmont Burn
ROSEMOUNT TERR
3
California Prim Sch
California
Quarryhead
FK1
76
2
rks
Gardrum
Gardrum Moss
1
Craigmad
Loch Ellrig
75
89
A
B
90
C
Blackbrigs

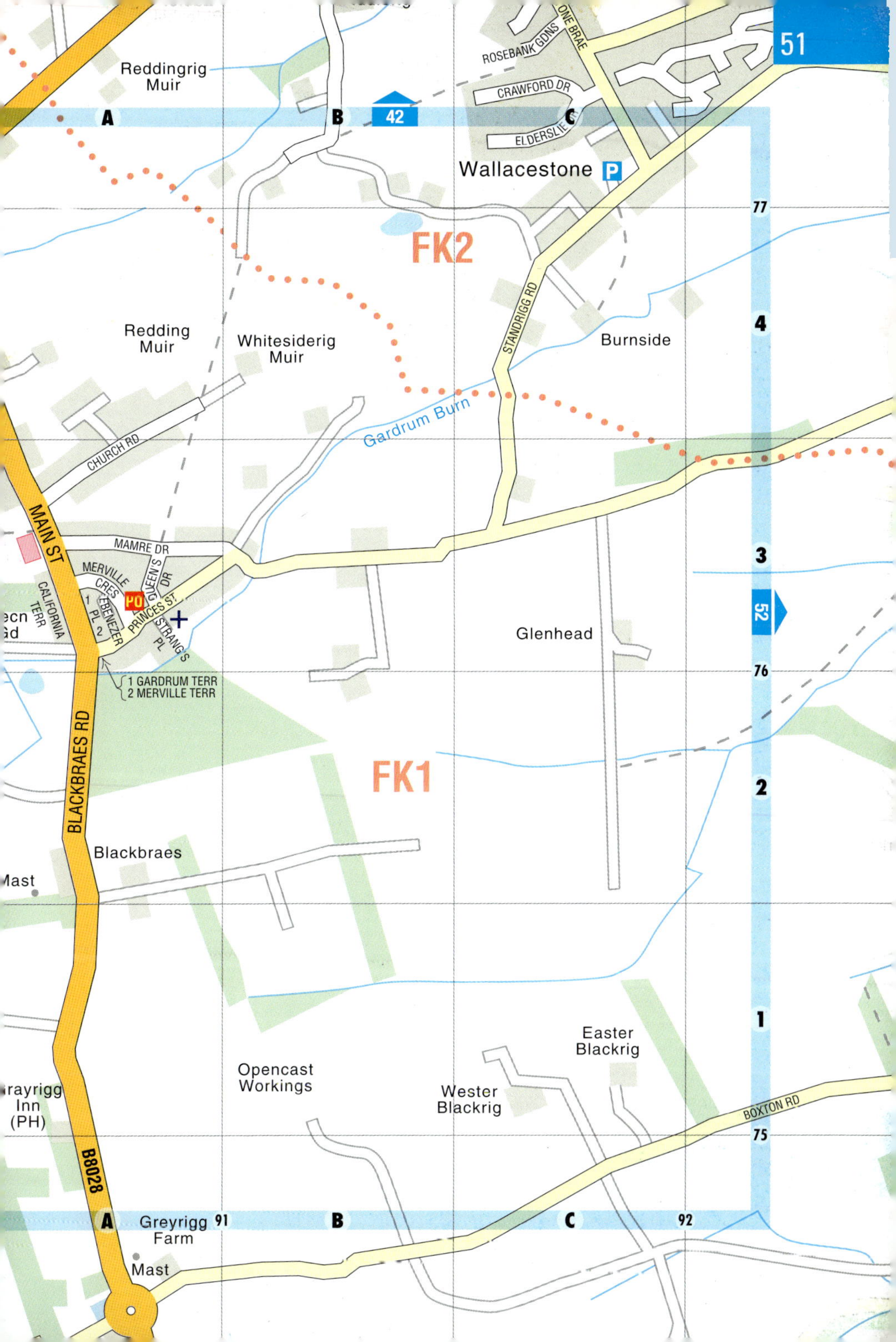

Reddingrig Muir
A
B
42
C
ROSEBANK GDNS
ONE BRAE
CRAWFORD DR
ELDERSLIE
Wallacestone
P
77
FK2
STANDRIGG RD
Redding Muir
Whitesiderig Muir
Burnside
4
Gardrum Burn
CHURCH RD
MAIN ST
MAMRE DR
MERVILLE CRES
QUEEN'S DR
PO
PRINCES ST
EBENEZER PL
CALIFORNIA TERR
STRANG'S PL
3
52
Glenhead
76
1 GARDRUM TERR
2 MERVILLE TERR
BLACKBRAES RD
FK1
2
Blackbraes
Mast
1
Easter Blackrig
Opencast Workings
Wester Blackrig
Inn (PH)
BOXTON RD
75
B8028
A
Greyrigg Farm
91
B
C
92
Mast

Sch
DR
COMYN DR
STANDRIGG AVE
STANDRIGG GDNS
ARNEIL PL
SUNNYSIDE COTTS
SUNNYSIDE RD
COMELY PK
TERR
HANLON GDNS
SOUTH CRAIGS
CRAIGS RD
NICOLTON
CRAWFORD DR
ELDERSLIE DR
PENDER GDNS
WALLACELEA
A
43
B
C
CARRON TERR
B805
GREENHITHE TERR
BELLEVUE
GREENWELL TERR
GOODMAN PL
HARLINGTON PL
CARRON VIEW
P
Wallacestone
77
STANDRIGG RD
Gardrum Burn
Greenwells
HAMILTON CRES
MACARTHUR CRES
CAIRNEY
BLACKMOUNT TERR
FK2
4
Burnside
BETHESDA GR
ANDERSON GDNS
RIGG
MANUEL
INGRAM PL
JAMES SMITH AVE
Manuel Burn
3
51
Glenhead
76
2
Works
FK1
Craigend
Snabhead
1
Easter Blackrig
BOXTON RD
75
Drumbowie Prim Sch
IRENE TERR
B825
92
A
Standburn
B
93
C

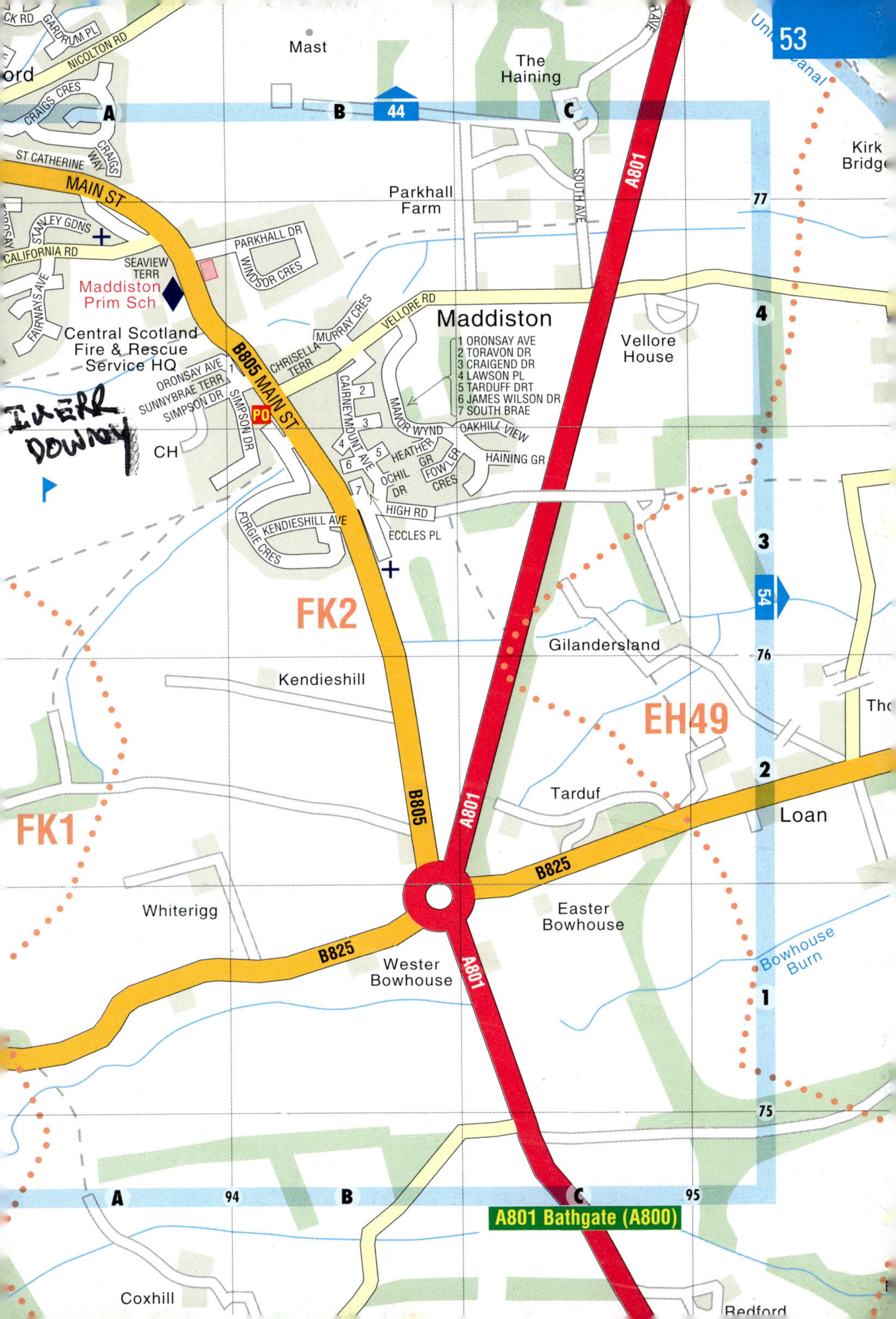
Mast
The Haining
Union Canal
Kirk Bridge
CK RD
GARDRUM PL
NICOLTON RD
CRAIGS CRES
CRAIGS WAY
ST CATHERINE
MAIN ST
STANLEY GDNS
CALIFORNIA RD
FAIRWAYS AVE
SEAVIEW TERR
Maddiston Prim Sch
Central Scotland Fire & Rescue Service HQ
PARKHALL DR
WINDSOR CRES
Parkhall Farm
SOUTH AVE
A801
MURRAY CRES
VELLORE RD
CHRISELLA TERR
Maddiston
1 ORONSAY AVE
2 TORAVON DR
3 CRAIGEND DR
4 LAWSON PL
5 TARDUFF DRT
6 JAMES WILSON DR
7 SOUTH BRAE
Vellore House
B805 MAIN ST
ORONSAY AVE
SUNNYBRAE TERR
SIMPSON DR
PO
CAIRNEYMOUNT AVE
MANOR WYND
OAKHILL VIEW
HEATHER GR
FOWLER CRES
OCHIL DR
HAINING GR
HIGH RD
CH
KENDIESHILL AVE
FORGIE CRES
ECCLES PL
FK2
Gilandersland
Kendieshill
EH49
FK1
Tarduf
B805
Loan
B825
Whiterigg
Easter Bowhouse
Wester Bowhouse
Bowhouse Burn
Coxhill
Redford
A801 Bathgate (A800)
A B C
44
54
77 76 75
94 95
4 3 2 1

The Haining
A
45
B
C
Kirk Bridge
FK2
Whitecross Ind Pk
SOUTH AVE
77
Cemy
Union Canal
HAINING VALLEY STEADINGS
4
Manuel Burn
Vellore House
A801
Gilmeadowland
ALMOND RD
Almond
B825
3
53
EH49
Gilandersland
76
Compston
Thornloan
2
Tarduf
Loan
Muiravonside Country Park
B825
Castlehill
Easter Bowhouse
Bowhouse Burn
1
FK2
Muiravonside Wood
75
95
A
B
96
C
A706 Bathgate (A801, A800)
A801
River Avon
Redford

Bo'ness Junction
Easter Manuel
PRIORY PL
PRIORY RD
HAINING RD
AVON RD
STATION RD
REYNARD GDNS
BAYNE GDNS
CARRIBBER AVE
ALMOND TERR
PO
HAINING TERR
MANUEL TERR
AVONTOUN CRES
1 COCKBURN CRES
2 SANDYFORD AVE
Prim Sch
McLAREN AVE
Manuelhaugh
B825
Avon Viaduct
River Avon
BURNSIDE GDNS
Whitecross
Sewage Wks
Mill
Manuel House
EH49
Woodcockdale
A706
Works
Avon Aqueduct
Kettlestoun Lower Wood
CRAIGS CHALET PK
Belsyde
Kettlestounhills
Muiravonside House
Carribber Glen
Easter Carribber
Carribber Reservoir
WATERSIDE
WESTVIEW
BURGH MILLS LA
TELFORD VIEW
A
B
C
97
98
77
76
75
4
3
2
1

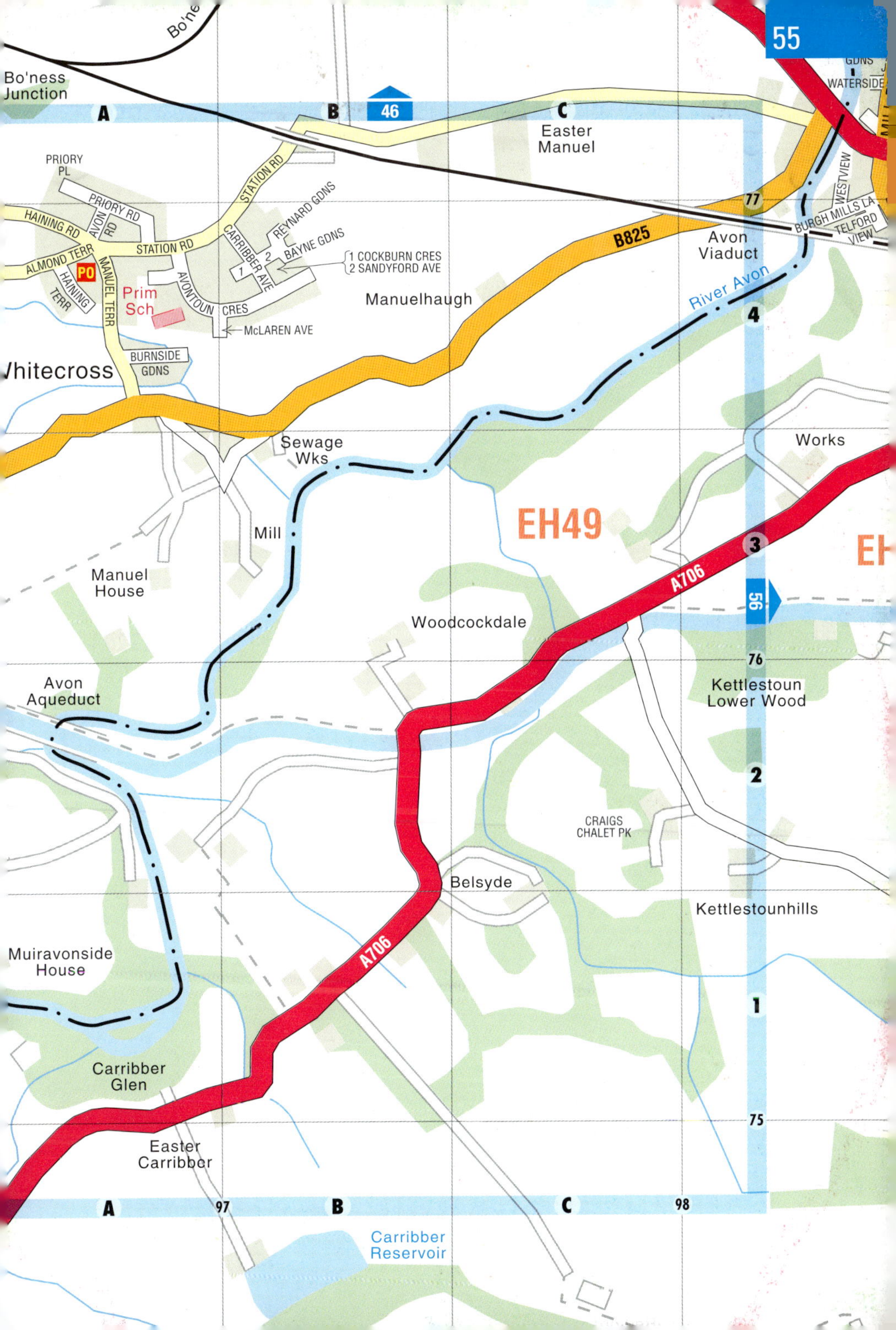

46
56

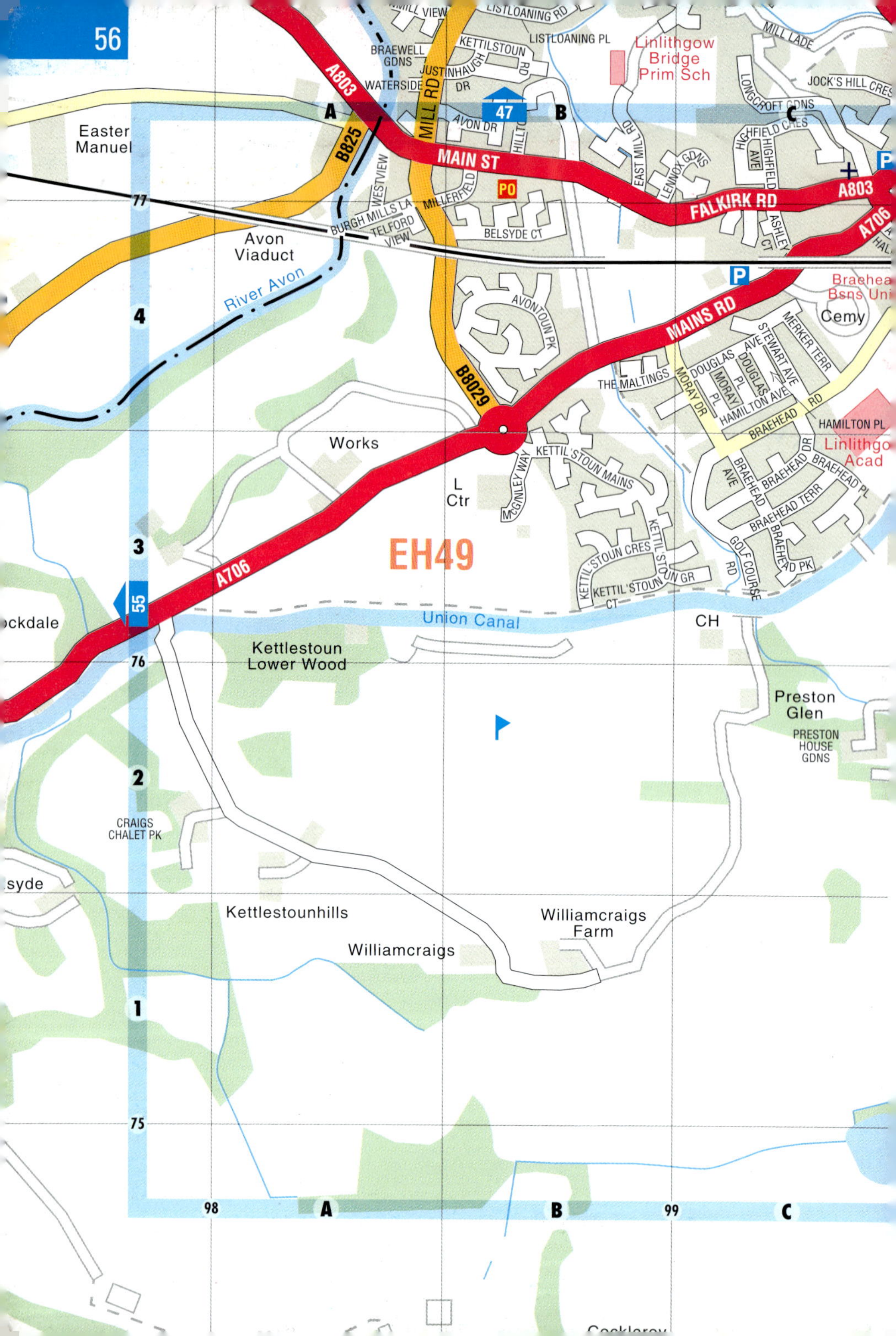

Easter Manuel
Avon Viaduct
River Avon
Works
L Ctr
EH49
Union Canal
Kettlestoun Lower Wood
CH
Preston Glen
PRESTON HOUSE GDNS
CRAIGS CHALET PK
Kettlestounhills
Williamcraigs
Williamcraigs Farm
Linlithgow Bridge Prim Sch
Braehead Bsns Uni
Cemy
HAMILTON PL
Linlithgo Acad
MAIN ST
FALKIRK RD
MAINS RD
MILL RD
A803
A706
B825
B8029
47
55
BRAEWELL GDNS
WATERSIDE
JUSTINHAUGH DR
KETTILSTOUN RD
LISTLOANING RD
LISTLOANING PL
MILL LADE
JOCK'S HILL CRES
LONGCROFT GDNS
HIGHFIELD CRES
HIGHFIELD AVE
AVON DR
EAST MILL RD
LENNOX GDNS
WESTVIEW
MILLERFIELD
BURGH MILLS LA
TELFORD VIEW
BELSYDE CT
ASHLEY CT
AVONTOUN PK
THE MALTINGS
MORAY DR
MORAY PL
DOUGLAS AVE
DOUGLAS PL
STEWART AVE
MERKER TERR
HAMILTON AVE
BRAEHEAD RD
BRAEHEAD AVE
BRAEHEAD DR
BRAEHEAD PL
BRAEHEAD TERR
BRAEHEAD PK
GOLF COURSE RD
KETTIL'STOUN MAINS
KETTIL'STOUN CRES
KETTIL'STOUN GR
KETTIL'STOUN CT
McGINLEY WAY
77
76
75
98
99
A
B
C
1
2
3
4

Linlithgow Loch
1 HAMILTON PK
2 ST JOHN'S AVE
Low Port Prim Sch
TH
Liby
THE VENNEL
Mus
KIRKGATE
MARKET LA
48
A803
HIGH ST
HIGH PORT
PO
Ct
ST NINIAN'S RD
A706
ST NINIAN'S WAY
WATER YETT
WHITTEN LA
WEST PORT
WYND
NEW WELL
UNION RD
WEST PORT PL
ST MICHAELS LA
BARONS HILL AVE
BARONS HILL CT
PROVOST RD
REGENT SQ
MADDERFIELD MEWS
B9080
EDINBURGH RD
MAIDLANDS
HILLSIDE COTTS
ST MAGDALENES
BACK STATION RD
Linlithgow
Union Canal
STRAWBERRY BANK
MANSE RD
ROYAL TERR
AVON PL
CANAL TERR
Linlithgow Canal Ctr
St Michael's
PRESTON CT
BARKHILL RD
PRESTON AVE
PRESTON TERR
PRESTON CRES
PRESTON PK
ROCKVILLE GR
CLARENDON CRES
CLARENDON RD
FRIARS BRAE
1 BURGESS HILL
2 PRIORY RD
FRIARS LOAN
Friar's Brae
Clarendon House
LINLITHGOW
Linlithgow Prim Sch
PRESTON RD
PRIORY RD
RIVALDSGREEN CRES
WALDIE AVE
FRIARS WAY
OATLANDS PK
DEANBURN PK
DEANBURN RD
DEACONS CT
LAVEROCK PK
RICCARTON RD
CARMELAWS
EH49
ACREDALES
BEECHWOOD
THE GLEBE
Dark Entry
Parkley Craigs
Preston House
Hiltly
Cauldhame
Upper Glen
HILLHOUSE FARM STEADINGS
Beecraigs Country Park Visitor Ctr
A
B
C
00
01
77
76
75
4
3
2
1

Index

Street names are listed alphabetically and show the locality, the Postcode district, the page number and a reference to the square in which the name falls on the map page

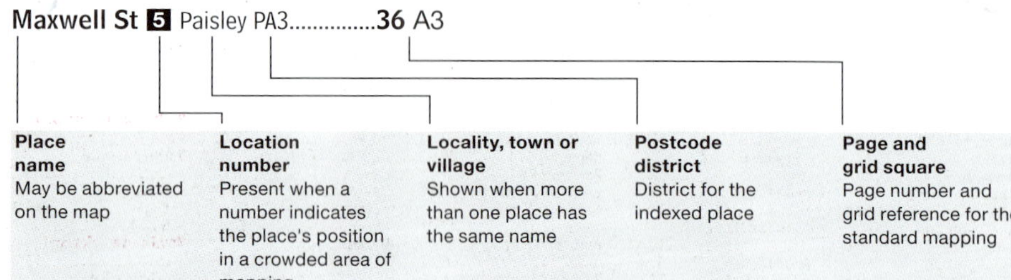

Towns and villages are listed in CAPITAL LETTERS
Public and commercial buildings are highlighted in magenta. **Places of interest** are highlighted in blue with a star★

Abbreviations used in the index

Acad	**Academy**	Ct	**Court**	Hts	**Heights**	Pl	**Place**
App	**Approach**	Ctr	**Centre**	Ind	**Industrial**	Prec	**Precinct**
Arc	**Arcade**	Ctry	**Country**	Inst	**Institute**	Prom	**Promenade**
Ave	**Avenue**	Cty	**County**	Int	**International**	Rd	**Road**
Bglw	**Bungalow**	Dr	**Drive**	Intc	**Interchange**	Recn	**Recreation**
Bldg	**Building**	Dro	**Drove**	Junc	**Junction**	Ret	**Retail**
Bsns, Bus	**Business**	Ed	**Education**	L	**Leisure**	Sh	**Shopping**
Bvd	**Boulevard**	Emb	**Embankment**	La	**Lane**	Sq	**Square**
Cath	**Cathedral**	Est	**Estate**	Liby	**Library**	St	**Street**
Cir	**Circus**	Ex	**Exhibition**	Mdw	**Meadow**	Sta	**Station**
Cl	**Close**	Gd	**Ground**	Meml	**Memorial**	Terr	**Terrace**
Cnr	**Corner**	Gdn	**Garden**	Mkt	**Market**	TH	**Town Hall**
Coll	**College**	Gn	**Green**	Mus	**Museum**	Univ	**University**
Com	**Community**	Gr	**Grove**	Orch	**Orchard**	Wk, Wlk	**Walk**
Comm	**Common**	H	**Hall**	Pal	**Palace**	Wr	**Water**
Cott	**Cottage**	Ho	**House**	Par	**Parade**	Yd	**Yard**
Cres	**Crescent**	Hospl	**Hospital**	Pas	**Passage**		
Cswy	**Causeway**	HQ	**Headquarters**	Pk	**Park**		

Index of towns, villages, streets, hospitals, industrial estates, railway stations, schools, shopping centres, universities and places of interest

1st–All

1st St
Grangemouth, Chemical Works FK3 ....35 A4
Grangemouth, Oil Refinery FK3 ....18 C1
2nd St
Grangemouth, Chemical Works FK3 ....35 A4
Grangemouth, Oil Refinery FK3 ....18 C2
3rd St
Grangemouth, Chemical Works EH51 ....35 A4
Grangemouth, Oil Refinery FK3 ....18 C2
4th St
Grangemouth, Chemical Works EH51 ....35 B4
Grangemouth, Oil Refinery FK3 ....19 A2
5th St
Grangemouth, Chemical Works EH51 ....35 B4
Grangemouth, Oil Refinery FK3 ....19 A2
6th St
Grangemouth, Chemical Works EH51 ....35 B4
Grangemouth, Oil Refinery FK3 ....19 A2
7th St
Grangemouth, Chemical Works EH51 ....35 B3
Grangemouth, Oil Refinery FK3 ....19 B2
8th St FK3, EH51.....19 B2

A

Abbots Ct FK2 ......15 C1
Abbotsford Dr
Grangemouth FK3 ....33 C4
Laurieston FK2 ......32 A2
Abbotsford Gdns FK2 ....15 A3
Abbotsford St FK2 ....15 A2
Abbotsgrange Rd FK3 ....18 A1
Abbotsinch Ct FK3 ....18 B1
Abbotsinch Ind Est FK3 ....18 B1
Abbotsinch Rd FK3 ....18 B1
Abbots Moss Dr FK1 ....40 A3
Abbots Rd
Falkirk, Bankside FK2 ....15 C2
Falkirk, Middlefield FK2 ....15 C1
Grangemouth FK3....17 C1
Abbots Road Rdbt FK2 ....15 C2
Abbots View FK2....33 C1
Abercairney Cres FK2 ....52 C4
Abercairney Pl FK3 ....18 A1
Abercrombie St FK1 ....29 B4
Academy Rd EH51 ....21 B1
Acorn Cres FK5.....13 C3
Acredales EH49.....57 B3
Acre Rd EH51.......39 A4
Acre View EH51.....38 C4
Adam Cres FK5.....14 B4
Adam Grossert Ct FK5 ....5 C1
Adams Loan FK2....14 C3
Adam St FK2........31 A4
Affric Dr FK2.......15 B3
Afton Dr FK6........9 C1
Ailsa Ct 3 FK2......44 A1
Ainslie Gdns FK2....33 C1
Airlie Dr FK2........44 A4
Airthrey Dr FK5......6 B2
Aitchison Dr FK5.....5 A1
Aitchison Pl FK1....30 B1
Aitken Gdns FK1....29 B4
Aitken Rd FK1 .....29 A4
Aitken Terr FK1 .....29 A4
Akarit Rd FK5.......14 A4
Albert Ave FK3......18 B2
Albert Rd FK1.......30 A1
Alder Gr FK2........32 B1
Alexander Ave
Falkirk FK2 ....31 B3
Grangemouth FK3....32 C3
Allanbank Rd FK5...13 B4
Allan Barr Ct FK1 ...40 C3
Allan Cres FK6.......2 C1
Allan Ct FK3........18 A3

Alloa Rd FK5 6 B2
Alloway FK2 32 A2
Alloway Cres FK4 25 C4
Alloway Wynd FK5 5 B2
Alma La FK2 30 B4
Alma St FK2 30 B4
Alma Terr FK2 30 B4
Almond Ct FK2 16 A1
Almond Rd
Falkirk FK2 16 A1
Whitecross EH49 54 B3
Almond St FK3 32 C4
Almond Terr EH49 55 A4
Alpha St EH51 35 B3
Alyth Dr FK2 44 B3
Amberley Path FK3 33 C4
Amulree Pl EH51 20 B1
Anderson Ave 2 FK2 14 C2
Anderson Cres FK1 50 C4
Anderson Dr
Denny FK6 10 A3
Falkirk FK2 15 A4
Anderson Gdns FK2 52 C4
Anderson Park Rd FK6 10 B4
Anderson St FK4 26 B3
Anderson Terr FK4 24 B1
Andrew Cres FK5 5 C2
Angus Rd EH51 37 A4
Annan Ct FK1 41 A3
Anne Dr FK5 6 A2
Annet Rd FK6 25 A4
Annfield Pl FK3 17 C2
Anson Ave FK1 29 B2
Antonine Ct EH51 37 A3
Antonine Gdns FK1 28 C3
Antonine Gr FK4 25 C1
Antonine Prim Sch FK4 26 A2
Antonine St FK1 28 C3
Antonine Wall★ FK4 27 A2
ANTONSHILL 6 A2
Antonshill Rdbt FK5 6 B3
Appin Gr FK2 33 C1
Arbuthnot St FK1 29 B4
Archibald Russell Ct FK2 43 C3
Ard Ct FK3 33 A3
Ardgay Cres FK4 26 A1
Ardgay Dr FK4 26 A1
Ardgay Rd FK4 26 A1
Ardgay Terr FK4 26 A1
Ardmore Dr FK2 44 B3
Ardvreck Pl FK2 6 C1
Argyll Ave FK2 30 C4
Argyll Path FK6 9 C2
Armour Mews FK5 5 A2
Arneil Pl FK2 43 B1
ARNOTHILL 30 A2
Arnothill FK1 30 A2
Arnothill Bank FK1 30 A2
Arnothill Ct FK1 29 C3
Arnothill Gdns FK1 30 A2
Arnothill La 1 FK1 29 C2
Arnothill Mews FK1 30 A2
Arnot St FK1 30 C2
Arran Ct FK3 33 A4
Arran Terr FK1 28 C2
Arthur's Dr FK5 14 B4
Ashcroft Ho FK5 13 A3
Ash Gr
Stenhousemuir FK5 14 B4
Westquarter FK2 42 C4
Ashley Ct EH49 56 C4
Ashley Hall Gdns EH49 56 C4
Ashley Rd FK2 33 C1
Ashley St FK4 25 C4
Athol Cres FK2 32 A1
Atholl Pl FK2 30 C3
Atrium Way FK4 26 A1
Auchentyre Pl FK2 7 B1
Auchincloch Dr FK4 23 C1
Avalon Gdns EH49 47 B2
Aven Dr FK2 31 C1
Avenue The FK2 15 C4
Avonbank Ave FK3 33 B4
Avonbank Gdns FK6 2 C2
Avon Ct FK1 41 A4
Avondale Rd FK2 34 B1
Avondhu Gdns FK3 18 B2
Avon Dr EH49 47 B1
Avonlea Dr FK2 33 C1
Avonmill Rd EH49 47 A2
Avonmill View EH49 47 A1
Avon Pl
Bo'ness EH51 21 A2
Linlithgow EH49 57 B4
Avon Rd
Grangemouth EH51 19 C1
Whitecross EH49 55 A4
Avonside Dr FK6 2 C3
Avon St
Denny FK6 2 B2
Grangemouth FK3 16 C3
Avontoun Pk EH49 56 B4

B

Back Station Rd EH49 48 C1
Bailielands EH49 49 B1
BAINSFORD 15 A2
Bainsford Prim Sch FK2 15 A2
Baird St FK1 29 A3
Bairns Ford Ave FK2 14 C1
Bairns Ford Ct FK2 14 C1
Bairns Ford Dr FK2 14 C1
Baker St EH51 37 C4
Balfour Cres FK5 13 B4
Balfour St FK4 25 C4
Ballinkier Ave FK4 23 B1
Balmoral Dr FK1 29 B1
Balmoral Gdns FK2 43 B1
Balmoral Pl FK5 6 A2
Balmoral Rd EH51 35 B4
Balmoral St FK1 29 B1
Baltic Quay FK3 17 C3
BANKHEAD 25 B4
Bankhead Cres FK4 25 A4
Bankhill Ct FK3 33 A4
Bankier Prim Sch FK4 23 B1
Bankier Rd FK4 23 B1
Bankier Terr FK4 23 B1
BANKNOCK 23 B1
BANKSIDE 15 B2
Bankside FK2 15 B1
Bankside Ct FK6 10 A4
Bankside Ind Est FK2 15 C2
Bank St
Falkirk FK1 30 B3
Grangemouth FK3 16 C3
Bankview Terr FK4 25 B4
BANTASKIN 29 C2
Bantaskine Dr FK1 29 C2
Bantaskine Gdns FK1 29 B1
Bantaskine Prim Sch FK1 29 B2
Bantaskine Rd FK1 29 C2
Bantaskine St FK1 29 B1
Banton Pl FK4 26 A1
Baptie Pl EH51 37 B3
Barkhill Rd EH49 57 A4
Barkin Ct FK1 40 C4
Barleyhill FK4 26 B3
Barnego Rd FK6 2 C1
Barnton La FK1 30 B2
Barons Hill Ave EH49 48 C1
Barons Hill Ct EH49 48 C1
Barony Ct EH51 37 C3
Barra Pl FK5 6 C2
Barrie Pl FK3 33 A3
Barrie Rd FK5 6 B1
Battery Rd FK3 19 B2
Battock Rd FK2 44 A1
Baxter Cres FK6 9 B3
Baxter's Wynd FK1 30 B2
Bayne Gdns EH49 55 B4
Beach Rd FK3 19 A3
BEANCROSS 32 C2
Beancross Prim Sch FK3 32 C3
Beancross Rd FK3 32 C3
Beancross Rdbt FK3 32 B4
Bean Row FK1 30 B2
Bearcroft Gdns FK3 18 A1
Bearcroft Rd EH51 19 C2
Beaufort Dr FK2 6 C1
Beauly Ct
Falkirk FK1 41 A3
Grangemouth FK3 33 A2
Beaumont Dr FK2 15 A4
Beech Cres
Denny FK6 2 B1
Larbert FK5 13 B2
Westquarter FK2 32 B1
Beech Pl FK3 32 C4
Beechwood EH49 57 B3
Begg Ave FK1 29 B2
Bell Ct
Falkirk FK2 15 B1
Grangemouth FK3 18 A3
Bellevue FK2 43 C1
Bellevue St FK1 30 C2
Bells Burn Ave EH49 49 A1
Bellsdyke Hospl FK5 5 C3
Bellsdyke Rd
Falkirk FK2 7 B4
Stenhousemuir FK5 5 C2
Bellsdyke Rdbt FK5 5 A1
Bellsmeadow Rd FK1 30 C2
Bell's Wynd FK1 30 B2
Belmont Ave
Bonnybridge FK4 25 A3
Shieldhill FK1 41 C1
Belmont St FK1 30 C2
Belmont Twr FK1 30 C2
Belsyde Ct EH49 56 B4
Benjamin Dr EH51 37 B3
Berryhill Cres FK3 33 B4
Bethesda Gr FK2 52 C4
Binnie Pl FK2 16 B4
Birkhill Clay Mine★ EH49 45 C4
Birkhill Cres EH51 37 C4
Birkhill St EH51 37 C4
Birkhill Sta★ EH49 35 C1
Birnam Pl FK2 30 C3
Blackbraes Rd FK1 51 A2
Blackmill Cres FK2 7 A1
Blackmount Terr FK2 52 C4
Blackness Rd EH49 48 C1
Blaefaulds Cres FK6 9 C2
Blair Ave EH51 37 B3
Blairdenon Cres FK1 29 C1
Blairlodge Ave FK2 43 A2
Blair's Cotts FK2 43 A3
Blair Terr FK5 6 C2
Bleachfield FK2 30 A3
Blenheim Pl FK5 6 A3
Blinkbonny Rd FK1 29 B2
Bluebell Cl 15 FK1 30 B2
Bog Rd
Banknock FK4 23 B1
Laurieston FK2 31 C2
Bog Rdbt FK2 31 C2
Bog Road Ind Est FK2 31 C2
Bog The EH51 21 B2
Bo'mains Rd EH51 37 B4
Bomar Ave EH51 21 B2
BO'NESS 20 C2
Bo'ness Acad EH51 38 A4
Bo'ness Hospl EH51 20 C1
Bo'ness & Kinneil Rly★ EH51 20 A1
Bo'ness Public Sch (Prim) EH51 21 A1
Bo'ness Rd
Grangemouth FK3 34 B4
Polmont FK2 33 C1
Bo'ness Sta★ EH51 21 B2
Bonhard Ct EH51 38 B4
Bonhard Way EH51 38 B3
BONNYBRIDGE 26 B3
Bonnybridge Hospl FK4 26 C4
Bonnybridge Ind Est FK4 26 A2
Bonnybridge Prim Sch FK4 26 B4
Bonnybridge Rd FK4 25 B3
Bonnyfield Rd FK4 25 C3
Bonnyhill Rd
Bonnybridge FK4 27 A1
Falkirk FK1 28 A2
Bonnymuir Cres FK4 25 C3
Bonnyside Rd FK4 26 B3
Bonnytoun Ave EH49 49 A2
Bonnytoun Terr EH49 49 A2
Bonnyvale Pl FK4 25 C3
Bonnyview Gdns FK4 26 B4
Bonnywood Ave FK4 11 A1
Booth Pl FK1 30 B2
BORROWSTOUN 37 C3
Borrowstoun Cres EH51 37 C3
BORROWSTOUN MAINS 37 B3
Borrowstoun Pl EH51 37 C3
Borrowstoun Rd EH51 38 A3
Bothkennar Prim Sch FK2 8 B1
Bothkennar Rd FK2 8 A1
Boundary St EH51 21 C2
BOWHOUSE 33 B3
Bowhouse Prim Sch FK3 33 B3
Bowhouse Rd FK3 33 A3
Bowhouse Sq FK3 33 A3
Bowling Green Pl FK4 25 C3
Bowmains Ind Est EH51 37 C3
Boxton Rd FK1 52 A1
Boyd La FK2 30 B4
Boyd St
Falkirk FK2 30 B4
Laurieston FK2 32 A1
Bradbury St FK2 15 A4
Braeface Rd FK4 23 B1
Braefoot Rd EH51 38 A3
Braehead EH51 21 A1
Braehead Ave EH49 56 C3
Braehead Bsns Units EH49 56 C4
Braehead Dr EH49 56 C3
Braehead Gr EH51 21 A1
Braehead Pk EH49 56 C3
Braehead Pl EH49 56 C3
Braehead Rd EH49 56 C4
Braehead Terr EH49 56 C3
Braemar Cres FK2 30 C4
Braemar Dr FK2 30 C4
Braemar Gdns
Denny FK6 2 C1
Grangemouth FK2 43 B2
Braemar Pl FK5 6 C2
Brae Rd FK3, EH51 35 A4
Braes High Sch FK2 42 C2
Braeside FK1 50 B4
Braeside Pl
Grangemouth FK2 42 C2
Laurieston FK2 32 B2
Westquarter FK2 42 C4
Braes View
Denny FK6 9 C2
Shieldhill FK1 41 C1
Braeview
Laurieston FK2 31 C1
Stenhousemuir FK5 13 C4
Braewell Gdns EH49 47 A1
Bravo St EH51 35 B3
Breadalbane Pl FK2 44 B4
Brechin Dr FK2 44 B3
Breton Ct FK1 30 C1

Brewlands Ave EH51 . . . 37 A3
Brewster Pl FK6 . . . 9 B4
Briar Brae FK2 . . . 43 B2
Briardene FK2 . . . 32 A1
Bridge Cres FK6 . . . 9 C4
BRIDGENESS . . . 22 A2
Bridgeness Cres EH51 . . . 22 A1
Bridgeness La EH51 . . . 22 A1
Bridgeness Rd EH51 . . . 22 B1
Bridge Pl FK6 . . . 9 B4
Bridge St FK4 . . . 26 A3
BRIGHTONS . . . 43 A2
Broadside Pl FK6 . . . 9 C3
Broad St FK6 . . . 10 B4
Brodick Pl FK1 . . . 28 C2
Brodie St FK2 . . . 15 A2
Bronte Pl FK5 . . . 6 C1
Brooke La FK3 . . . 32 C3
Brooke St FK3 . . . 32 C3
Brookside FK2 . . . 43 C3
Broomage Ave FK5 . . . 5 A1
Broomage Bank FK5 . . . 13 B4
Broomage Cres FK5 . . . 5 A1
Broomage Dr FK5 . . . 5 A1
Broomage Pk FK5 . . . 13 B3
Broomhill Ave FK5 . . . 13 B2
Broomhill Pl FK6 . . . 2 C2
Broomhill Rd FK4 . . . 26 B2
Broompark Gdns FK6 . . . 10 A4
Broomridge Pl FK4 . . . 25 A2
Broomside Pl FK5 . . . 13 B3
Broomside Rd FK4 . . . 26 B1
Broomyhill Pl EH49 . . . 47 B1
Brosdale Ct FK1 . . . 40 C4
Brown Ct FK3 . . . 17 C2
Brownieknowe Pl FK2 . . . 14 B2
Brown St FK1 . . . 29 A3
Bruart Ave FK5 . . . 6 B1
Bruce Cres FK2 . . . 7 A1
Bruce Dr FK5 . . . 6 B1
Bruce Gdns 1 FK2 . . . 43 B2
Bruce Pl FK3 . . . 18 A2
Bruce Rd EH51 . . . 35 B3
Bruce St FK2 . . . 30 C4
Bryce Ave FK2 . . . 15 A4
Bryden Ct FK3 . . . 18 A2
Bryson Pl FK5 . . . 5 B3
Bryson St FK2 . . . 30 B4
Bryson Street Ind Est FK2 . . . 30 B4
Buchanan Ct
Bo'ness EH51 . . . 37 B3
Falkirk FK2 . . . 14 C2
Buchanan Gdns FK2 . . . 43 B4
Buchan Ave FK2 . . . 15 A3
Buchan Pl FK3 . . . 32 C3
Buchan Rd FK3, EH51 . . . 35 A4
Bulloch Cres FK6 . . . 9 C3
Bungalows The FK5 . . . 13 A3
Burder Pk FK2 . . . 14 C4
Burgess Hill EH49 . . . 57 B4
Burgh Mills La EH49 . . . 56 A4
Burghmuir Ct EH49 . . . 49 B2
Burnbank Rd
Falkirk FK2 . . . 15 A1
Grangemouth FK3 . . . 33 A3
Burnbrae Gdns FK1 . . . 30 A3
Burnbrae Rd FK1 . . . 30 A3
Burnfield Pl FK2 . . . 15 C1
Burnfoot Ct FK3 . . . 33 A4
Burnfoot La 1 FK1 . . . 30 B2
Burnhead La FK1 . . . 30 C2
Burnhead Rd FK5 . . . 5 B1
Burns Ave
Grangemouth FK3 . . . 33 A3
Stenhousemuir FK5 . . . 5 B3
Burns Cres FK2 . . . 31 C2
Burnside Ct FK1 . . . 29 B3
Burnside Gdns EH49 . . . 55 A4
Burnside Pl FK2 . . . 7 A1
Burnside Terr
Falkirk FK1 . . . 29 B3
Redding FK2 . . . 42 C3
Bute Pl FK3 . . . 33 A4
Bute St FK2 . . . 30 B4
By-Pass Rd FK4 . . . 25 B3

C

Cadell Dr FK2 . . . 6 C3
Cadzow Ave EH51 . . . 37 C4
Cadzow Cres EH51 . . . 21 A1
Cadzow La EH51 . . . 21 A1
Cairneymount Ave FK2 . . . 53 B4
Cairngorm Rd FK3 . . . 33 B3
Cairnoch Wlk FK6 . . . 9 C3
Cairn's La EH51 . . . 21 C1
Calder Pl FK1 . . . 41 B3
Caledonian Ct FK2 . . . 15 B1
Caledonia Terr FK4 . . . 25 C3
CALIFORNIA . . . 50 C3
California Prim Sch FK1 . . . 51 A3
California Rd
Maddiston FK2 . . . 53 A4
Shieldhill FK1 . . . 50 C4
California Terr FK1 . . . 51 A3
Callander Dr FK5 . . . 13 B2
Callendar Ave FK1 . . . 40 C3
Callendar Bsns Pk FK1 . . . 31 B1
Callendar Bvd FK1 . . . 31 B1
Callendar House* FK1 . . . 31 A1
Callendar Park Dr FK1 . . . 31 A2
Callendar Park Terr FK1 . . . 31 A2
Callendar Park View FK1 . . . 31 A2
Callendar Park Wlk FK1 . . . 31 A2
Callendar Rd FK1 . . . 31 A2
Callendar Riggs FK1 . . . 30 C2
Callendar Square Sh Ctr 5 FK1 . . . 30 B2
CAMELON . . . 28 C3
Camelon Ed Ctr FK1 . . . 29 B4
Camelon Rd FK1 . . . 29 C3
Camelon Rdbt FK1 . . . 29 A4
Camelon Sta FK1 . . . 29 A4
Cameron Pl FK2 . . . 15 A4
Campbell Cres FK2 . . . 31 C1
Campbell Dr FK5 . . . 13 A4
Campfield St FK2 . . . 30 B4
Campie Terr FK2 . . . 16 B4
Campsie Rd FK3 . . . 33 B3
Canal Bank Ind Est FK4 . . . 26 A2
Canal St
Falkirk, Camelon FK1 . . . 29 A3
Falkirk FK2 . . . 15 A1
Canal Terr EH49 . . . 57 B4
Canal Wlk FK2 . . . 43 A3
Canalyard Ind Est FK1 . . . 40 C3
Canavan Ct FK2 . . . 15 B1
Canavan Pk FK2 . . . 15 B1
Candie Cres FK3 . . . 33 B4
Candie Rd FK3 . . . 18 C2
Canmore Dr FK5 . . . 6 A2
Cannons Way FK2 . . . 14 C3
Carbrook Pl FK3 . . . 33 B4
Carbrook Terr FK5 . . . 5 B1
Carhowden Rd FK2 . . . 32 B1
Carmelaws EH49 . . . 57 B3
CARMUIRS . . . 28 B3
Carmuirs Ave FK1 . . . 28 C3
Carmuirs Dr FK1 . . . 28 B4
Carmuirs Prim Sch FK1 . . . 29 A3
Carmuirs St FK1 . . . 29 A3
Carnegie Dr FK1 . . . 29 A4
Carradale Ave FK1 . . . 28 C2
Carribber Ave EH49 . . . 55 B4
Carrick Pl
Falkirk FK2 . . . 6 C1
Falkirk, Tamfourhill FK1 . . . 28 C2
CARRIDEN . . . 22 A1
Carriden Brae EH51 . . . 39 A4
Carriden Glade EH51 . . . 22 B1
Carriden Ind Est EH51 . . . 22 C1
Carriden Pl EH51 . . . 38 C4
Carriden View EH51 . . . 38 C4
CARRON . . . 14 C4
Carronbank Ave FK2 . . . 15 A4
Carronbank Cres FK6 . . . 3 A1
Carronbank Ct FK2 . . . 15 A4
Carronflats Rd FK3 . . . 18 A2
Carrongrange Ave FK5 . . . 14 A4
Carrongrange Gdns FK5 . . . 14 A3
Carrongrange Gr FK5 . . . 14 A3
Carrongrange Rd FK5 . . . 14 A4
Carrongrange Sch FK5 . . . 14 A4
Carrongrove Ave FK2 . . . 14 C4
Carrongrove Bsns Pk FK2 . . . 14 C4
Carrongrove Rd FK2 . . . 14 C4
Carronhall Ave FK2 . . . 7 B2
Carronlea Dr FK2 . . . 14 C4
Carron Pl FK3 . . . 33 A2
Carron Prim Sch FK2 . . . 14 C4
Carron Rd
Falkirk FK2 . . . 14 C2
Falkirk FK2 . . . 14 C3
Carron Rdbt FK2 . . . 14 C4
CARRONSHORE . . . 7 B1
Carronshore Prim Sch FK2 . . . 7 B2
Carronshore Rd FK2 . . . 15 A4
Carronside Pl FK6 . . . 3 A1
Carronside St FK2 . . . 15 A2
Carron Terr FK2 . . . 43 C1
Carronvale Ave FK5 . . . 13 C3
Carronvale Rd
Larbert FK5 . . . 13 C2
Stenhousemuir FK5 . . . 13 B3
Carronview FK5 . . . 13 C4
Carron View FK2 . . . 43 C1
Carse Cres FK2 . . . 32 A2
Carse Knowe EH49 . . . 49 B1
Carse View EH51 . . . 37 A3
Castings Ave FK2 . . . 15 A1
Castings Ct
Falkirk FK2 . . . 15 A1
Falkirk, Middlefield FK2 . . . 31 B4
Castings Dr FK2 . . . 30 B4
Castings Ho FK2 . . . 15 A1
Castings Rd FK2 . . . 31 B4
Castle Ave FK2 . . . 7 B1
Castle Cres
Denny FK6 . . . 9 C4
Falkirk FK2 . . . 15 C1
Castle Ct FK2 . . . 15 B1
Castle Dr
Falkirk FK2 . . . 15 B2
Stenhousemuir FK5 . . . 14 B4
Castlehill EH51 . . . 37 A4
Castlelaurie Ind Est FK2 . . . 15 B1
Castlelaurie St FK2 . . . 15 B1
CASTLELOAN . . . 20 B1
Castle Pl FK2 . . . 15 C1
Castlerankine Rd FK6 . . . 9 B4
Castle Rd FK2 . . . 15 B2
Castle Terr FK6 . . . 9 B4
Castleton Cres FK3 . . . 33 A4
Castleview Terr FK4 . . . 24 A1
Cathrine Gr EH51 . . . 38 A3
Cedar Cres FK2 . . . 42 B4
Cedar Gr FK5 . . . 13 C3
Cedar St FK3 . . . 17 C1
Central Ave FK3 . . . 32 C3
Central Bvd FK5 . . . 5 A2
Central Dock Rd FK3 . . . 18 A4
Central Dr FK5 . . . 6 B1
Central Park Ave FK5 . . . 5 A2
Central Park Bsns Pk FK5 . . . 5 A2
Central Ret Pk FK1 . . . 30 C3
Centurion Way FK2 . . . 29 A4
Chacefield St FK4 . . . 26 A4
Chacefield Wood FK6 . . . 10 A1
Chalmers Bldg EH49 . . . 47 B1
Chambers Dr FK2 . . . 15 A4
Chapel Cres FK2 . . . 7 A1
Chapel Dr FK5 . . . 6 A1
Chapel La FK1 . . . 30 B3
Charing Cross 1 FK3 . . . 17 C3
Charles Dr FK5 . . . 13 B2
Charlotte Dundas Ct FK3 . . . 33 B4
Charlotte Hill Ct FK5 . . . 5 A1
Charlotte St FK2 . . . 43 B2
Chattan Ind Est FK4 . . . 26 C2
Checkbar Rdbt FK5 . . . 11 B1
Chestnut Cres FK6 . . . 2 B1
Chestnut Gr
Bo'ness EH51 . . . 36 C3
Stenhousemuir FK5 . . . 6 B1
Cheviot Pl FK3 . . . 33 B3
Chisholm Pl FK3 . . . 32 B4
Chrisella Terr FK2 . . . 53 B4
Christie Terr FK5 . . . 6 A1
Churchill Pl FK2 . . . 15 B1
Church La FK6 . . . 2 C1
Church Pl FK2 . . . 30 B4
Church Rd
Bo'ness EH51 . . . 20 C1
California FK1 . . . 51 A3
Church St
Bonnybridge FK4 . . . 26 C1
Falkirk FK2 . . . 15 B4
Stenhousemuir FK5 . . . 6 A1
Church Wlk FK6 . . . 10 A4
Church Wynd EH51 . . . 21 A1
Clanranald Pl FK1 . . . 40 A3
Claremont St FK4 . . . 25 C4
Clarendon Cres EH49 . . . 57 C4
Clarendon Rd EH49 . . . 57 C4
Claret Rd
Grangemouth, Bowhouse FK3 . . . 33 B4
Grangemouth, Oil Refinery FK3 . . . 19 B1
Clarinda Ave FK1 . . . 28 B3
Clarinda Pl FK5 . . . 5 B2
Clark Ave EH49 . . . 47 C2
Clover Pl EH51 . . . 37 B3
Cluny Dr FK5 . . . 6 B2
Clyde Cres FK5 . . . 5 A1
Clydesdale St EH51 . . . 37 C4
Clyde St
Falkirk FK1 . . . 29 B3
Grangemouth FK3 . . . 17 A3
Cobblebrae Cres FK2 . . . 15 A3
Cochrane Ave FK1 . . . 30 B2
Cochrane St FK1 . . . 30 B2
Cockburn Cres EH49 . . . 55 B4
Cockburn St FK1 . . . 30 B2
College Cres FK2 . . . 15 C1
Collingwood Ct FK1 . . . 29 B3
Coll Pl FK3 . . . 33 A4
Colonsay Ave FK2 . . . 43 B4
Colonsay Terr FK1 . . . 40 C4
Comely Park Gdns 17 FK1 . . . 30 B2
Comely Park Prim Sch FK1 . . . 30 B2
Comely Park Terr 14 FK1 . . . 30 B2
Comely Pk FK2 . . . 43 C1
Comely Pl FK1 . . . 30 B2
Comely Terr FK2 . . . 43 C1
Commissioner St EH51 . . . 21 B2
Compressor House Rd FK3 . . . 34 C3
Compton Rd FK3 . . . 32 C3
Comrie Terr EH51 . . . 37 C4
Comyn Dr FK2 . . . 43 A1
Conner Ave FK2 . . . 14 C2
Connolly Dr FK6 . . . 2 B2
Connolly Pl FK6 . . . 10 B3
Conroy Ct 1 FK6 . . . 10 A3
Conway Ct FK1 . . . 29 C2

Corbiehall EH51 ... 20 C1
Corentin Ct FK1 ... 30 C1
Corona Cres FK4 ... 25 C3
Coronation Pl FK2 ... 8 B1
Corporation St FK1 ... 30 C2
Corrie Ave FK5 ... 6 B2
Corrie Pl FK1 ... 28 C2
Cortachy Ave FK2 ... 6 C1
Cotland Dr FK2 ... 14 B2
Cottage Cres FK1 ... 29 B3
Cotton La FK2 ... 32 A1
Courtyard The FK1 ... 31 B1
Cowan St FK4 ... 26 A4
Cowden Hill Gdns FK4 ... 26 B4
Cowdenhill Rd EH51 ... 21 C1
Cow Wynd FK1 ... 30 B2
Craigallan Pk EH51 ... 21 C1
Craigburn Ct 4 FK1 ... 40 A4
Craigend Dr FK2 ... 53 B4
Craigie Ct FK5 ... 13 A4
Craigievar Ave FK2 ... 6 C1
Craiglaw Terr 3 FK2 ... 43 B2
Craigleith Rd FK3 ... 33 A4
Craigmillar Pl FK5 ... 6 B2
Craigs Chalet Pk EH49 ... 55 C2
Craigs Cres FK2 ... 44 A1
Craigs Terr FK2 ... 43 C1
Craigs Way FK2 ... 44 A1
Craigview EH51 ... 22 A1
Cramond Ct FK1 ... 40 C4
Cranshaws Dr FK2 ... 43 A4
Crathes Ave FK5 ... 6 C2
Crathie Dr FK6 ... 2 C1
Crawfield Ave EH51 ... 37 A4
Crawfield La EH51 ... 37 C3
Crawfield Rd EH51 ... 37 B2
Crawford Dr FK2 ... 42 C1
Creran Dr FK6 ... 25 A4
Creteil Ct FK1 ... 30 C1
Creteil Pl FK3 ... 17 C2
Crichton Dr FK3 ... 18 A2
Cricket Pl FK2 ... 43 A3
Crimond Pl FK1 ... 41 C1
Crockett Pl FK2 ... 15 A2
Croft Est FK4 ... 24 B1
Croftfoot Pl FK6 ... 2 C2
Crofthead St FK2 ... 14 B2
Croftside Ct FK3 ... 33 B4
Cromwell Dr FK1 ... 31 A2
Cromwell Rd FK1 ... 31 A2
Cromwell Rd W FK1 ... 31 A2
Cross Brae FK1 ... 50 B4
Crossgatehead Rd FK2 ... 43 B2
Crosshall Pl FK1 ... 50 B4
Crosshill Dr EH51 ... 37 C3
Cross St FK2 ... 15 A3
Cross The EH49 ... 48 B1
Crownest Loan FK5 ... 14 A4
Cruachan Ct FK1 ... 41 A4
Cruachan Pl FK3 ... 33 C3
Cruden Rd EH51 ... 35 A3
Cruickshank Dr FK1 ... 50 B4
Cruikshank's Ct 3 FK6 ... 10 A3
Cuffabouts EH51 ... 22 B1
Cuillin Ct FK1 ... 41 A3
Cuillin Pl FK3 ... 33 B3
Culduie Circ FK2 ... 44 B3
Culmore Pl FK1 ... 41 C3
Cultenhove Cres FK3 ... 33 B4
Culvain Pl FK1 ... 41 A4
Culzean Pl FK5 ... 6 B2
Cumbernauld Rd FK4 ... 24 A1
Cumbrae Dr FK1 ... 28 C2
Cunningham Gdns FK2 ... 31 C3
Cunningham Rd FK5 ... 6 C1
Cunningham St FK3 ... 32 C4
Custonhall Pl FK6 ... 9 C4
Cuttyfield Pl FK2 ... 7 B1

D

Daintree Terr FK1 ... 29 B3
Dalderse Ave FK2 ... 30 B4
Dalgrain Ind Est FK3 ... 17 B3
Dalgrain Rd FK3 ... 17 A3
Dalratho Rd FK3 ... 18 A2
Darian La EH51 ... 21 A1
Davaar Pl FK1 ... 28 C2
David's Loan FK2 ... 15 C3
Davies Row FK6 ... 10 A4
Dawson Pl EH51 ... 37 B3
Dawson St FK2 ... 15 A2
Deacons Ct EH49 ... 57 B3
Deanburn Gr EH51 ... 37 A4
Deanburn Pk EH49 ... 57 A3
Deanburn Prim Sch EH51 ... 37 A3
Deanburn Rd EH49 ... 57 A3
Deanburn Wlk EH51 ... 37 A4
DEANFIELD ... 20 B1
Deanfield Cres EH51 ... 20 C1
Deanfield Dr EH51 ... 37 B4
Deanfield Pl EH51 ... 20 C1
Deanfield Rd EH51 ... 20 C1
Deanfield Terr EH51 ... 37 B4
Deangate Gdns EH51 ... 37 A4
Dean Rd EH51 ... 37 B4
Demoreham Ave FK6 ... 10 B3
DENNY ... 10 B3
Denny High Sch FK6 ... 10 A2
DENNYLOANHEAD ... 25 A3
Denny Prim Sch FK6 ... 9 C4
Denny Rd
Denny FK4 ... 25 B4
Larbert FK5 ... 12 C3
Denovan Rd FK6 ... 3 A2
Derwent Ave FK1 ... 29 C2
Devon St FK3 ... 16 C3
Dickburn Cres FK4 ... 25 C3
Dobbie Ave
Larbert FK5 ... 13 B2
Stenhousemuir FK5 ... 13 B3
Dochart Cres FK2 ... 44 A4
Dochart Path FK3 ... 33 A3
Dochart Pl FK1 ... 41 B4
Dock Rd FK3 ... 17 C3
Dock St
Bo'ness EH51 ... 21 B2
Falkirk FK2 ... 15 B4
Dog Well Wynd EH49 ... 48 B1
Dollar Ave FK2 ... 14 C1
Dollar Gdns FK2 ... 14 C1
Dollar Ind Est FK1, FK2 ... 30 A3
Don St FK3 ... 16 C3
Doocot Brae EH51 ... 21 C1
Dorrator Ct FK1 ... 29 B3
Dorrator Rd FK1 ... 29 B4
Douglas Ave
Grangemouth, Bowhouse FK3 ... 33 B4
Grangemouth, Brightons FK2 ... 43 B2
Linlithgow EH49 ... 56 C4
Douglas Dr EH51 ... 37 B4
Douglas Pl
Bo'ness EH51 ... 37 C4
Linlithgow EH49 ... 56 C4
Stenhousemuir FK5 ... 6 B2
Douglas Rd EH51 ... 37 C4
Douglas Terr EH51 ... 37 C4
Doune Cres FK5 ... 6 C2
Dovecot Pk EH49 ... 49 B2
Dovecot Rd FK2 ... 42 B4
Dower Cres EH51 ... 21 C2
Drossie Rd FK1 ... 30 A1
Drove Loan FK6 ... 25 C4
Drove Loan Cres FK6 ... 10 A1
Drumacre Rd EH51 ... 38 B4
Drum Cotts EH51 ... 38 C4
Drum Farm La EH51 ... 38 C4
Drumlanrig Pl FK5 ... 6 B2
Drummond Pk FK3 ... 33 B4
Drummond Pl
Bonnybridge FK4 ... 10 C1
Falkirk FK1 ... 40 A4
Grangemouth FK3 ... 18 A2
Drumpark Ave EH51 ... 38 B4
Drum Rd EH51 ... 38 C4
Drumside Terr EH51 ... 22 A1
Drumview Gdns EH51 ... 38 A3
Dryburgh Ave FK6 ... 9 C4
Dryburgh Way FK3 ... 33 C4
Duchess Anne Cotts EH51 ... 36 C4
Dugald Stewart Ave EH51 ... 21 B1
Duke St
Denny FK6 ... 9 B4
Grangemouth FK3 ... 18 B2
Dumyat Dr FK1 ... 29 B1
Dumyat Rise FK5 ... 5 B3
Dunavon Gdns FK6 ... 2 C2
Dunbar Ave FK5 ... 6 B2
Dunbar Gate FK6 ... 3 A1
Duncairn Ave FK4 ... 25 C4
Duncan Ave FK2 ... 7 A1
Duncan St FK4 ... 25 C3
Duncarron Ind Est FK6 ... 10 B3
Duncarron Pl FK6 ... 10 A4
Dundaff Ct FK6 ... 9 C3
Dundarroch St FK5 ... 13 A3
Dundas Cres FK2 ... 32 A1
Dundas Rd FK2 ... 32 A2
Dundas St
Bo'ness EH51 ... 21 A1
Grangemouth FK3 ... 17 B2
Dundee Ct 5 FK2 ... 14 C2
Dundee Pl FK2 ... 14 C2
DUNIPACE ... 2 C2
Dunipace Prim Sch FK6 ... 2 C1
Dunkeld Pl FK2 ... 15 B3
Dunning Pl FK2 ... 15 B3
Dunnottar Dr FK5 ... 6 B2
Dunrobin Ave FK5 ... 6 B3
Dunure Cres FK4 ... 26 A3
Dunure St FK4 ... 26 A3
Dunvegan Ave FK5 ... 6 B2
Dunvegan Dr FK2 ... 15 B3
Dunvegan Pl
Bonnybridge FK4 ... 25 C4
Polmont FK2 ... 44 B3

E

Earl's Gate Rdbt FK3 ... 16 C1
Earl's Rd FK3 ... 17 A2
Earn Ct FK3 ... 33 A3
Earn Pl FK6 ... 25 A4
East Boreland Pl FK6 ... 2 C1
East Bridge St FK1 ... 30 C2
Eastburn Dr FK1 ... 30 C2
Eastburn Twr FK1 ... 30 C2
Eastcroft Dr FK2 ... 44 B4
Eastcroft St FK5 ... 13 A3
East Dr FK5 ... 13 B3
Easter Carmuirs Prim Sch FK1 ... 28 B4
East Mill Rd EH49 ... 47 B1
Easton Dr FK1 ... 41 B1
East Pier St EH51 ... 21 A2
East Rd FK3 ... 34 C3
Ebenezer Pl FK1 ... 51 A3
Eccles Pl FK2 ... 53 B3
Edinburgh Rd EH49 ... 48 C1
Edward Ave FK5 ... 6 A2
Edward Pl FK2 ... 8 B1
Eighth St FK3, EH51 ... 19 B2
Elam Terr EH51 ... 20 C1
Elderslie Dr FK2 ... 42 C1
Elgin Pl FK1 ... 30 C2
Elim Dr FK1 ... 50 A4
Elizabeth Ave
Grangemouth FK3 ... 18 A2
Stenhousemuir FK5 ... 13 B4
Elizabeth Cres FK1 ... 28 B4
Elliot Terr FK2 ... 14 C2
Elmbank Cres FK4 ... 25 A4
Elmbank St FK3 ... 32 C4
Elm Dr FK2 ... 42 B4
Elm Gr FK5 ... 13 C3
Emma's Way FK4 ... 25 C3
Endrick Dr FK6 ... 25 B4
Epworth Gdns FK2 ... 42 C2
Erbach Ave FK2 ... 32 B2
Ercall Rd FK2 ... 43 C2
Eriskay Ct FK1 ... 41 A4
Erngath Rd EH51 ... 21 B1
Erskine Hill FK2 ... 43 C3
Estate Ave FK1 ... 30 C2
Etive Way FK2 ... 44 B4
Etna Ct FK2 ... 15 C1
Etna Rd FK2 ... 15 C1
Etna Road Rdbt FK2 ... 16 A1
Ettrick Ct
Falkirk FK1 ... 41 B3
Grangemouth FK3 ... 33 C4
Evans St FK5 ... 5 B1
Evergreen Trailer Ct FK6 ... 10 C4
Ewart Gr EH51 ... 37 C3
Ewing Ave FK2 ... 15 A1
Ewing Dr FK2 ... 15 A1
Ewing Pl FK2 ... 15 A1

F

Fairfield Ave FK4 ... 26 A4
Fairfield Pl FK2 ... 30 C3
Fairhaven Terr FK2 ... 42 B2
Fairlie Dr FK1 ... 29 A3
Fairlie Gdns FK1 ... 29 A3
Fairlie St FK1 ... 28 C3
Fairspark Terr EH51 ... 37 A3
Fairways Ave FK2 ... 53 A4
Fairways Pl FK4 ... 11 A1
Falcon Dr FK5 ... 5 A1
FALKIRK ... 31 A4
Falkirk & District Royal Infmy FK1 ... 30 A2
Falkirk Grahamston Sta FK1 ... 30 B3
Falkirk High Sch FK1 ... 29 B2
Falkirk High Sta FK1 ... 30 A1
Falkirk Rd
Bonnybridge FK4 ... 26 C4
Falkirk FK2, FK3 ... 31 C4
Falkirk, Glen Village FK1 ... 40 C3
Larbert FK5 ... 13 A3
Larbert FK5 ... 13 B2
Linlithgow EH49 ... 47 C1
Falkirk Stadium (Falkirk FC) FK2 ... 31 C4
Falkirk Wheel (Rotating Boat Lift)★ FK1 ... 28 A3
Falkland Pl FK5 ... 6 A2
Farm St FK2 ... 14 C3
Farmstead Way EH51 ... 38 C4
Farquharson Way FK1 ... 40 A3
Fendoch Rd FK3 ... 18 B1
Ferguson Dr
Denny FK6 ... 9 C3
Falkirk FK2 ... 6 C3
Ferguson Gr FK4 ... 26 B4
Fern Lea Gr FK2 ... 7 B1
Fifth St
Grangemouth, Chemical Works EH51 ... 35 B4
Grangemouth, Oil Refinery FK3 ... 19 A2
Findhorn Pl FK1 ... 41 B4
Finistere Ave FK1 ... 30 B1
Finlarig Ct FK5 ... 6 B2
Finlayson Pl FK5 ... 5 B3
Fintry Rd FK3 ... 33 B3
Fir Gr FK2 ... 42 C4
Fir La FK5 ... 13 C3
Firs Pk (East Stirlingshire FC) FK2 ... 30 C4
Firs St FK2 ... 30 C4
First St
Grangemouth, Chemical Works FK3 ... 35 A4
Grangemouth, Oil Refinery FK3 ... 18 C1
Firwood Dr EH51 ... 37 A3
Fishers' Rd EH49 ... 37 A1
Flare Rd FK3 ... 34 B3
Fleming Ct FK6 ... 9 C2
Fleming Dr FK5 ... 6 C1
Fleming Gdns FK1 ... 29 B4
Fleming St FK6 ... 10 A3
Forbes Cres FK5 ... 13 C3

Forbes Ct FK2 ...... 31 B4
Forbes Rd FK1 ...... 31 A2
Ford Rd FK4 ...... 26 A3
Fordyce Gdns FK1 ...... 29 B2
Foredale Terr EH51 ...... 22 B1
Forest View FK2 ...... 44 A3
Forfar Pl FK2 ...... 44 B3
Forgie Cres FK2 ...... 53 B3
Forrester Gait FK5 ...... 4 A4
Forth Ave FK5 ...... 5 A1
Forth St FK3 ...... 17 C2
Forth Terr FK3 ...... 17 C2
Forth Valley Coll Falkirk FK2 ...... 31 B4
Forthview Cres EH51 ...... 37 A4
Forthview Ct 5 FK1 ...... 40 A4
Forthview Gdns FK2 ...... 43 A2
Forthview Terr FK2 ...... 42 C2
Forties Rd FK3, EH51 ...... 35 A3
Fortingall Cres FK2 ...... 44 B4
Fortuna Ct FK1 ...... 30 C2
Foundry Loan FK5 ...... 13 A4
Foundry Rd FK4 ...... 26 B3
Foundry St FK2 ...... 14 C2
Fountainpark Cres EH51 ...... 22 A1
Fourth St
Grangemouth, Chemical Works EH51 ...... 35 B4
Grangemouth, Oil Refinery FK3 ...... 19 A2
Fowler Cres
Denny FK6 ...... 10 A3
Maddiston FK2 ...... 53 B3
Fowler Pl FK2 ...... 33 B1
Foxdale Ave FK4 ...... 26 A1
Foxdale Ct FK4 ...... 26 A1
Foxdale Dr FK4 ...... 26 A1
Foxdale Pl FK4 ...... 26 A1
Franchi Dr FK5 ...... 6 B3
Fraser Pl FK3 ...... 33 A4
Friars Brae EH49 ...... 57 B4
Friars Loan EH49 ...... 57 B4
Friars Way EH49 ...... 57 B3
Friendship Gdns FK2 ...... 7 B1
Frobisher Ave FK1 ...... 29 C2
Fullerton Dr FK2 ...... 33 B1
Fulmar Cres FK5 ...... 5 B3
Furnace La EH51 ...... 22 A2

G

Gairdoch Dr FK2 ...... 7 B1
Gairdoch St FK2 ...... 15 A2
Gairloch Cres FK2 ...... 43 A4
Galloway Ct FK1, FK2 ...... 30 B4
Galloway St FK1 ...... 30 B4
Gallowsknowe EH49 ...... 47 B1
Gardenhead FK2 ...... 44 A4
Garden St FK1 ...... 30 C3
Garden Terr
Falkirk FK1 ...... 30 C3
Westquarter FK2 ...... 42 B4
Gardrum Gdns FK1 ...... 41 B1
Gardrum Pl FK2 ...... 44 A1
Gardrum Terr FK1 ...... 51 A3
Garngrew Rd
Haggs FK4 ...... 23 C1
Longcroft FK4 ...... 24 A1
Garrison Pl FK1 ...... 30 B3
Garry Pl
Falkirk FK1 ...... 41 B4
Grangemouth FK3 ...... 33 B3
Gartcows Ave FK1 ...... 30 A2
Gartcows Cres FK1 ...... 30 A1
Gartcows Dr FK1 ...... 30 A2
Gartcows Gdns 5 FK1 ...... 29 C2
Gartcows Pl FK1 ...... 30 A1
Gartcows Rd FK1 ...... 30 A1
Garthill Gdns FK1 ...... 30 A2
Garthill La FK1 ...... 30 A2
Garvald La FK6 ...... 9 B3
Garvald Rd FK6 ...... 9 C1
Gascoigne Ct 8 FK2 ...... 14 C2
Gateside Ave FK4 ...... 26 C4
Gateway Bsns Pk FK3 ...... 32 C3
Gauze Ct EH51 ...... 38 A4
Gauze Pl EH51 ...... 38 A4
Gauze Rd EH51 ...... 38 A4
George Laing Ct FK5 ...... 14 A4
George St
Bo'ness EH51 ...... 37 C4
Falkirk FK2 ...... 30 B3
Grangemouth FK3 ...... 18 B2
Laurieston FK2 ...... 31 C1
Stenhousemuir FK5 ...... 5 B1
Gerald Terr FK5 ...... 6 A1
Gibbdun Pl FK6 ...... 10 A1
Gibsongray St FK2 ...... 14 C1
Gibson St FK6 ...... 10 A3
Gilburn Pl EH51 ...... 37 A4
Gilchrist Dr FK1 ...... 29 B2
Gilfillan Pl FK2 ...... 15 B4
Gill Pk FK6 ...... 10 A4
Gilsay Ct FK1 ...... 41 A4
Gilston Cres FK2 ...... 44 B3
Gladstone Rd FK5 ...... 5 C1
Glamis Gdns FK2 ...... 44 A3
Glasgow Rd
Denny FK6 ...... 10 A3
Falkirk FK1 ...... 28 C4
Longcroft FK4 ...... 24 C2
Glebe St
Denny FK6 ...... 10 A4
Falkirk FK1 ...... 30 B3
Glebe The EH49 ...... 57 B3
Gledhill Ave EH51 ...... 39 A3
Glenard View EH51 ...... 39 A4
Glen Avon Pl FK2 ...... 44 A1
Glenbank FK1 ...... 40 C3
Glenbervie FK5 ...... 4 C2
Glenbervie Ave FK5 ...... 4 C1
Glenbervie Cres FK5 ...... 5 A1
Glenbervie Dr FK5 ...... 4 C1
Glenbervie Rd FK3 ...... 33 C4
Glenbo Dr FK6 ...... 10 A1
Glen Brae FK1 ...... 30 A1
Glenbrae Ct FK1 ...... 30 B1
Glenburn Rd FK1 ...... 41 B3
Glenburn Way EH51 ...... 37 A3
Glencairn St FK1 ...... 28 B3
Glen Cres FK1 ...... 40 C3
Glenfuir Ct FK1 ...... 29 A2
Glenfuir Rd FK1 ...... 29 B3
Glenfuir St FK1 ...... 28 C3
Glengarry Cres FK1 ...... 40 A4
Glen Gdns FK1 ...... 30 A1
Glen Lyon Ct FK2 ...... 44 B4
Glenmore Dr FK4 ...... 25 C4
Glenochil Rd FK1 ...... 30 A1
Glen Ogle Ct FK2 ...... 44 B4
GLENSBURGH 16 C3
Glensburgh Rd FK3 ...... 16 C2
Glenside Ct FK3 ...... 33 B4
Glen Terr FK6 ...... 9 C3
Glen View
Bo'ness EH51 ...... 37 A2
Bonnybridge FK4 ...... 25 A3
Glenview Ave FK4 ...... 23 C1
Glenview Dr FK1 ...... 40 A4
GLEN VILLAGE 40 C3
Glowrorum Dr FK6 ...... 10 A1
Glynwed Ct FK2 ...... 15 B1
Godfrey Ave FK6 ...... 9 C3
Godfrey Cres FK5 ...... 13 B3
Golf Course Rd EH49 ...... 56 C3
Goodman Pl FK2 ...... 43 C1
Goosedubs Pl FK2 ...... 14 B2
Gordon Pl FK1 ...... 29 B3
Gorrie St FK6 ...... 9 C4
Gort Pl FK3 ...... 32 C3
Goshen Pl FK5 ...... 14 A4
Gowan Ave FK2 ...... 30 B4
Gowan La FK2 ...... 30 B4
Gradlon Pl FK1 ...... 30 B1
Graeme High Sch FK1 ...... 31 B2
Graham Ave FK5 ...... 5 A1
Graham Cres EH51 ...... 21 C1
Grahamsdyke Ave EH51 ...... 21 C1
Grahamsdyke Cres FK4 ...... 26 A1
Grahamsdyke La EH51 ...... 21 C1
Grahamsdyke Pl EH51 ...... 38 B4
Grahamsdyke Rd
Bo'ness EH51 ...... 38 C4
Bonnybridge FK4 ...... 26 A2
Grahamsdyke St
Laurieston FK2 ...... 31 C2
Laurieston FK2 ...... 32 A2
Grahamsdyke Terr EH51 ...... 21 C1
Grahams Rd FK1 ...... 30 B4
Grahams Road Rdbt FK1 ...... 30 B3
GRAHAMSTON 30 A4
Grampian Cres FK3 ...... 33 B3
Granary Rd FK2 ...... 14 C2
Granary Sq FK2 ...... 15 A1
Grange Ave FK2 ...... 31 A4
Grangeburn Rd FK3 ...... 18 A3
Grange Dr FK2 ...... 31 A4
Grange Knowe EH49 ...... 49 B2
Grange La FK3 ...... 17 B3
Grangelea Ct FK3 ...... 18 A2
Grange Loan EH51 ...... 21 C1
GRANGEMOUTH 17 A1
Grangemouth Ent Ctr FK3 ...... 16 C1
Grangemouth High Sch FK3 ...... 33 B3
Grangemouth Mus★ FK3 ...... 17 C3
Grangemouth Rd
Bo'ness EH51 ...... 36 B4
Falkirk FK2 ...... 31 B3
Grangemouth EH51 ...... 35 A3
GRANGEPANS 21 B1
Grangepans EH51 ...... 21 C2
Grange Pl
Grangemouth FK3 ...... 17 C2
Redding FK2 ...... 43 A3
Grange Prim Sch EH51 ...... 21 C1
Grange Rd FK3 ...... 33 C2
Grange Terr EH51 ...... 21 C1
Grange The FK2 ...... 43 C2
Grange View
Linlithgow EH49 ...... 49 A2
Stenhousemuir FK5 ...... 14 A3
Gray Buchanan Ct FK2 ...... 43 B4
Greenacre Dr FK4 ...... 26 A1
Greenacre Pl FK4 ...... 26 A1
Greenacre Rd FK4 ...... 26 A1
GREENBANK 28 C1
Greenbank Ct FK1 ...... 29 A2
Greenbank Pl FK1 ...... 29 A2
Greenbank Rd
Falkirk, Greenbank FK1 ...... 29 A1
Falkirk, Summerford FK2 ...... 29 A2
Greencraig Ave FK1 ...... 50 A4
Greenfield St FK4 ...... 26 B4
Greenhill Rd FK4 ...... 26 A1
Greenhithe Terr FK2 ...... 43 C1
Greenhorn's Well Ave 3 FK1 ...... 29 C1
Greenhorn's Well Cres 1 FK1 ...... 29 C1
Greenhorn's Well Dr 2 FK1 ...... 29 C1
Green La FK3 ...... 18 A2
Greenmount Dr FK1 ...... 50 A4
Greenpark Dr FK2 ...... 43 C4
Greens The FK2 ...... 52 C4
Green Tree La EH51 ...... 37 A3
Greenvale Dr FK2 ...... 43 C2
Greenwells Dr FK2 ...... 44 A2
Greenwell Terr FK2 ...... 43 C1
Grenville Ct FK1 ...... 29 C2
Griffiths St FK1 ...... 30 B2
Grove Cres FK2 ...... 14 C4
Grove St FK6 ...... 9 B4
Gunner Rd FK3, EH51 ...... 19 B2
Gunn Rd FK3 ...... 32 C3

H

Hadrian Way EH51 ...... 38 B4
HAGGS 24 A1
Haig St FK3 ...... 32 C4
Haining Gr FK2 ...... 53 C3
Haining Pl FK3 ...... 18 B2
Haining Rd EH49 ...... 55 A4
Haining Terr EH49 ...... 55 A4
Haining Valley Steadings EH49 ...... 54 C4
Halket Cres FK2 ...... 15 B4
HALLGLEN 41 B3
Hallglen Prim Sch FK1 ...... 40 C3
Hallglen Rd FK1 ...... 40 C3
Hallglen Terr FK1 ...... 40 C3
Hamilton Ave
Linlithgow EH49 ...... 56 C4
Stenhousemuir FK5 ...... 6 A2
Hamilton Cres FK2 ...... 52 C4
Hamilton Dr FK1 ...... 30 A2
Hamilton La EH51 ...... 21 A2
Hamilton Pk EH49 ...... 57 A4
Hamilton Pl EH49 ...... 56 C4
Hamilton Rd
Grangemouth FK3 ...... 33 B4
Stenhousemuir FK5 ...... 5 C4
Hamilton Sq EH51 ...... 37 A3
Hamilton St FK1 ...... 29 A4
Haney's Way EH51 ...... 21 C2
Hanlon Gdns FK2 ...... 43 C1
Hanover Grange FK3 ...... 17 C2
Harbour Rd EH51 ...... 22 A1
Harley Ct FK2 ...... 15 A2
Harlington Pl FK2 ...... 43 C1
Harlow Ave FK2 ...... 43 B3
Harrison Pl FK1 ...... 29 C3
Harris Pl FK3 ...... 32 C3
Hartley Pl FK3 ...... 32 B4
Harvey Ave FK2 ...... 44 A4
Haugh Gdns FK2 ...... 15 A3
Haugh St FK2 ...... 15 A3
Haughs Way FK6 ...... 10 A4
Hawley Rd FK1 ...... 31 A2
Hawthorn Dr
Denny FK6 ...... 2 C1
Falkirk FK1 ...... 29 B2
Hawthorne Pl FK5 ...... 13 C3
Hawthorn St FK3 ...... 32 C4
Hayfield FK2 ...... 15 B1
Hayfield Rd FK2 ...... 15 B1
Hayfield Terr FK6 ...... 10 A1
Haygate Ave FK2 ...... 43 C2
Haypark Bsns Ctr FK2 ...... 43 C4
Haypark Rd FK6 ...... 25 A4
Hayworth Ave FK2 ...... 32 B2
Hazel Cres FK6 ...... 2 C1
Hazeldean Ave EH51 ...... 37 A3
Hazel Gr FK2 ...... 15 C1
Hazelhurst FK2 ...... 43 C2
Hazel Rd FK3 ...... 32 C4
HEAD OF MUIR 25 B4
Head of Muir Prim Sch FK6 ...... 25 A4
Heather Ave FK1 ...... 50 A4
Heatherdale Gdns FK6 ...... 10 A1
Heather Gr FK2 ...... 53 B3
Hedges The FK1 ...... 29 B3
Hendry St FK2 ...... 15 A1
Henry St
Bo'ness EH51 ...... 38 A3
Grangemouth FK3 ...... 18 A2
Herbertshire St
Denny FK6 ...... 10 A4
Denny FK6 ...... 10 B4
Herdshill Ave FK1 ...... 50 A4
Heriot Gdns FK2 ...... 43 B3
Heritage Dr FK2 ...... 6 C1
Heugh St FK1 ...... 30 A1
HIGH BONNYBRIDGE 26 C1
Highfield Ave EH49 ...... 47 C1
Highfield Cres EH49 ...... 47 C1
Highland Dr FK5 ...... 5 B1
Highland Dykes Cres FK4 ...... 26 A4
Highland Dykes Dr FK4 ...... 26 B4
High Port EH49 ...... 48 C1
High Rd FK2 ...... 53 B3
High St
Bonnybridge FK4 ...... 26 A3
Falkirk FK1 ...... 30 B2
Linlithgow EH49 ...... 48 B1

High Station Ct FK1 30 A1
High Station Rd FK1 30 A1
High View Gr FK1 50 B4
Hillary Rd FK5 14 A3
Hillcrest EH51 37 C3
Hillcrest Pl FK6 9 C1
Hillcrest Rd 1 FK1 40 A4
Hillhead Ave FK4 23 B1
Hillhead Dr FK1 40 A4
Hillhouse Farm Steadings EH49 57 C1
Hillhouse Rd FK6 10 A1
Hillock Ave FK2 43 A4
Hillside Cotts EH49 49 A1
Hillside Gr EH51 38 C4
Hillside Terr FK2 32 B1
Hilltop EH49 47 B1
Hillview Rd
Bonnybridge FK4 26 C1
5 Grangemouth FK2 43 B2
Stenhousemuir FK5 5 B1
Hodge St FK1 30 B2
Hollandbush Ave FK4 23 B1
Hollandbush Cres FK4 23 C1
Holly Ave FK5 6 B1
Holmlea Ave 2 FK2 43 B2
Holyrood Pl FK5 6 A2
Home Farm Cotts FK6 25 C4
Hookney Terr FK6 9 B4
Hope Cotts EH51 39 A3
Hopepark Terr FK4 25 C4
Hope St
Bo'ness EH51 21 A2
Falkirk FK1 30 B3
Hornbeam Cres FK2 32 A1
Howard St FK1 29 C2
Howgate Sh Ctr 6 FK1 30 B2
Howieson Ave EH51 37 C3
Howie's Pl FK1 28 B2
Huntburn Ave EH49 49 A1
Hunter Gdns
Bonnybridge FK4 26 A3
Denny FK6 9 C4
Hunter Pl FK2 6 C2
Hurworth St FK1 29 C1

I

Icehouse Brae N FK2 32 B2
Icehouse Brae S FK2 32 B2
Inch Colm Ave FK5 5 B2
Inches Rdbt FK5 5 B2
Inches The FK3 18 A2
Inch Garvie Terr FK5 5 B2
Inchkeith Pl FK1 40 C4
Inchyra Pl FK3 33 C4
Inchyra Rd FK3 33 B3
Ingleston Ave FK6 2 C2
Inglis Dr FK2 15 B4
Inglis Pl FK2 43 C2
Ingram Pl FK2 52 C4
Innerpeffray Dr FK2 6 C1
Inverary Dr FK5 6 B3
Inveravon Rdbt EH51 35 A3
Iona Pl FK1 40 C4
Irving Ct FK1 29 B3
Islands Cres FK1 40 C4
Islay Ct FK3 33 A3
Ivybank Ct FK2 43 C4

J

Jackson Ave FK3 17 C1
Jacob Pl FK1 30 B1
James Cornwall Ct FK3 33 C4
James Croft Dr FK1 40 A3
James Smith Ave FK2 52 C4
James St
Falkirk FK2 30 B4
Laurieston FK2 31 C1
Laurieston FK2 32 A1
Longcroft FK4 24 A1
Stenhousemuir FK5 13 C4
James Watt Ave EH51 21 B1
James Wilson Dr FK2 53 B3
Jamieson Ave
Bo'ness EH51 37 B4
Stenhousemuir FK5 6 A1
Jarvie Pl 6 FK2 14 C2
Jasper Ave FK2 32 A2
Jeffrey Bank EH51 21 A1
Jeffrey Terr FK2 44 A4
Jessfield Pl EH51 37 C3
Jock's Hill Cres EH49 47 C1
John Bassy Dr FK4 23 A1
John Davidson Dr FK6 2 B2
John O'Hara Ct FK1 29 A3
John St
Falkirk FK2 15 A1
Longcroft FK4 24 A1
Johnston Ave FK5 6 B1
Johnston Ct 7 FK2 14 C2
Johnston Pl FK6 9 B3
Jones Ave FK5 13 B2
Jubilee Rd FK6 3 A1
Jubilee Way FK4 25 C3
Jura Pl FK3 33 A3
Justinhaugh Dr EH49 47 B1

K

Karries Ct FK6 9 A2
Katrine Pl FK6 25 A4
Keir Hardie Ave FK2 32 A1
Kelly Dr FK6 3 A1
Kelt Rd
Banknock FK4 23 B2
Longcroft FK6 24 A4
Kelty Ave EH51 21 B1
Kelvin St FK3 16 C3
Kemper Ave FK1 30 C1
Kendieshill Ave FK2 53 B3
Kenilworth Dr FK2 31 C2
Kenilworth La FK3 32 C3
Kenilworth St FK3 33 A3
Kenmore Ave FK2 44 B4
Kenmuir St FK1 28 A3
Kenmure Pl FK5 6 B2
Kennard Rd FK2 43 A2
Kennard St FK2 30 C4
Kenneil Mus & Roman Fortlet★ EH51 36 C4
Keppock Pl FK1 40 A3
Kerr Cres FK4 24 A1
Kerr Pl FK6 9 C4
Kerse Gdns FK2 31 B3
Kersehill Circ FK2 15 B1
Kersehill Cres FK2 15 B1
Kerse La FK1 30 C2
Kerse Pl FK1 30 C3
Kerse Rd FK3 17 C2
Kersiebank Ave FK3 33 B4
Kestrel Dr FK2 43 C1
Kettil'stoun Cres EH49 56 B3
Kettil'stoun Ct EH49 56 B3
Kettil'stoun Gr EH49 56 B3
Kettil'stoun Mains EH49 56 B3
Kettilstoun Rd EH49 47 B1
Kilbirnie Terr FK6 2 C1
Kilbrennan Dr FK1 28 B2
Kildrummy Ave FK5 6 B2
Killin Dr FK2 44 B4
Kilmory Ct FK1 28 C2
Kilns Pl FK2 29 C4
Kilns Rd FK1 30 A3
Kilsland Terr EH51 20 B1
Kilsyth Rd
Banknock FK4 23 A1
Longcroft FK4 24 A1
Kinacres Gr EH51 22 B1
Kincardine Rd FK2 7 B1
Kinglass Ave EH51 21 B1
Kinglass Ct EH51 38 A4
Kinglass Dr EH51 38 A4
Kinglass Pk EH51 38 A3
Kings Ct
7 Falkirk FK1 30 B2
Stenhousemuir FK5 13 C4
Kingseat Ave FK3 33 A4
Kingseat Pl FK1 29 C1
Kingsfield EH49 49 B2
Kingsley Ave FK5 6 B1
Kings Rd FK3 18 B2
King St
Falkirk FK2 30 C4
Stenhousemuir, Antonshill FK5 6 B1
Stenhousemuir FK5 13 C4
Kinloch Pl FK3 33 B3
Kinnaird Ave FK2 7 A1
Kinnaird Dr FK5 6 A1
KINNEIL 37 A3
Kinneil Dr EH51 37 A4
Kinneil Prim Sch EH51 37 C4
Kinneil Rd EH51 20 B1
Kinneil Sta★ EH51 20 B1
Kintyre Pl FK1 28 C2
Kirk Ave FK5 14 A4
Kirkgate EH49 48 B1
Kirkhall Pl FK6 10 A4
Kirkland Dr FK6 9 A4
Kirkslap FK6 10 A4
Kirkton Pl FK2 7 B1
Kirkwood Ave FK2 43 A4
Kirk Wynd 2 FK1 30 B2
Knights Way FK6 9 B4
Knowehead Rd FK2 43 A4

L

Lade Ct EH49 47 C1
Lade Dr FK5 13 B2
Lade Rd FK4 26 A3
Ladeside Cres FK5 14 A3
Ladeside Prim Sch FK5 13 B2
Ladysgate Ct FK2 7 A1
Ladysmill FK2 31 A3
Ladysmill Ind Est FK1 30 C3
Ladywell Ct FK5 4 C1
Ladywell View EH51 37 A3
Lafferty Pl FK6 10 B3
Lairox Terr FK6 2 C1
Lamond View FK5 13 C3
Langhill Pl FK6 9 B3
LANGLEES 15 C3
Langlees Prim Sch FK2 15 A2
Langlees St FK2 15 B3
Langton Rd FK2 32 A1
La Porte Prec 5 FK3 17 C3
LARBERT 13 A4
Larbert High Sch FK5 14 A3
Larbert Rd FK4 26 B4
Larbert Sta FK5 13 B4
Larbert Village Prim Sch FK5 13 A3
Larch Gr FK5 6 B1
Larch St FK3 32 C4
Lathallan Dr FK2 43 C4
Laurelbank Ave FK4 26 A1
Laurel Ct
Denny FK6 2 C1
Falkirk FK1 28 C4
Laurel Gr
Bonnybridge FK4 25 C1
Westquarter FK2 42 B4
Laurel Pl FK4 25 C1
LAURIESTON 32 B2
Laurieston Ind Est FK2 31 C1
Laurieston Prim Sch FK2 32 A1
Laurieston Rd FK3 32 A4
Laurmont Ct FK2 32 A1
Laverock Pk EH49 57 B3
Lawers Cres FK2 44 B3
Lawers Pl FK3 33 B3
Law Pl FK6 10 A3
Lawrence Ct FK5 5 A3
Lawson Pl FK2 53 B3
Laxdale Dr FK6 9 C1
Leapark Dr FK4 25 C1
Learmonth St FK1 30 B2
Lec Ct FK2 31 C2
Lecropt Sch (Barnardo's) FK1 28 C4
Ledi Pl FK1 41 C1
Ledmore Pl FK1 41 C3
Leishman Twr FK1 30 C2
Leith Pl FK6 9 C1
Lendrick Ave FK1 40 A4
Lennox Gdns EH49 47 B1
Lennox Terr FK3 33 C3
Leven St FK2 15 A2
Lewis Ct FK1 40 C4
Lewis Rd FK2 44 A3
Library La 7 FK3 17 C3
Liddle Dr EH51 37 B3
Lime Gr
Polmont FK2 43 C4
Stenhousemuir FK5 13 C3
Lime Rd FK1 28 B2
Lime St FK3 32 C4
Linden Ave FK6 2 B1
Links Ct EH51 21 B2
Links Pl EH51 21 C1
Links Rd EH51 21 B2
Linlithgow Acad EH49 56 C3
LINLITHGOW BRIDGE 47 B2
Linlithgow Bridge Prim Sch EH49 47 B1
Linlithgow Canal Ctr★ EH49 57 B4
Linlithgow Palace★ EH49 48 B1
Linlithgow Pl FK5 6 A2
Linlithgow Prim Sch EH49 57 A4
Linlithgow Rd EH51 37 C4
Linlithgow Sta EH49 48 C1
Linlithgow Story Mus The★ EH49 48 B1
Lint Riggs FK1 30 B3
Lionthorn Rd FK1 40 A3
Lion Well Wynd EH49 48 A1
Lismore Ct FK1 40 C4
Listloaning Pl EH49 47 B1
Listloaning Rd EH49 47 B1
Lithgow Pl FK6 9 B2
Little Carriden EH51 39 A3
Little Denny Rd FK6 9 C3
Livingstone Cres FK2 31 B3
Livingstone Dr
Bo'ness EH51 37 A4
Laurieston FK2 42 A4
Livingstone Terr FK2 42 C3
LOAN 54 A2
Loanhead Ave
Denny FK4 25 A4
Grangemouth FK3 33 B4
Loan The EH51 37 A4
Lochaber Dr FK5 6 A1
Lochgreen Rdbt FK1 40 A4
Lochhead Ave FK6 10 A3
Lochinvar Pl FK4 26 C1
Lochlands Ave FK5 13 A2
Lochlands Bsns Pk FK5 13 A2
Lochlands Ind Est FK5 12 C2
Lochlands Loan FK5 13 A1
Lochmaben Dr FK5 6 B2
Lochpark Pl FK6 10 A4
Lochridge Pl FK6 9 C3
Lochside Cotts FK2 42 C4
Lochside Cres FK2 42 C4
Lock Sixteen FK1 29 A3
Lodge Dr FK5 14 B4
Logie Dr FK5 4 C1
Lomond Cres FK5 6 B1
Lomond Dr FK2 15 B3
Lomond Rd FK3 33 B3
Lomond Way FK6 25 A4
Loney Cres FK6 10 A2
LONGCROFT 24 B1
Longcroft Gdns EH49 47 C1
Longcroft Holdings FK4 24 B1
Longdales Ave FK2 14 C2
Longdales Ct FK2 14 C2

Longdales Pl FK2 14 C2
Longdales Rd FK2 14 C2
Longdyke Pl FK2 7 B2
Lorimar Pl FK2 15 A4
Lorne Gdns FK2 31 C1
Lorne Rd FK5 13 B4
Lothian Cres EH51 38 A4
Lothian St EH51 38 A4
Loudens Wlk FK6 2 C3
Lovells Glen EH49 47 A2
Low Port Prim Sch EH49 48 B1
Lumley Ct FK3 17 C2
Lumley Pl FK3 17 C2
Lumley St FK3 17 C2
Lyall Cres FK2 43 C4
Lyness Ct FK2 43 C4
Lyon Ct EH51 37 A4

M

MacAdam Pl FK1 29 A4
MacArthur Cres FK2 52 C4
McCambridge Pl FK5 5 B3
MacDonald Ct FK5 5 A3
Macfarlane Cres FK1 30 B3
McGhee Pl FK1 40 A4
McGinley Way EH49 56 B3
Machrie Ct FK1 28 C2
Macintosh Pl FK1 40 B3
McKell Ct FK1 30 A1
McKenzie Pl 7 FK1 40 A4
Mackenzie Terr FK3 32 C4
MacLachlan Ave FK6 9 B3
McLachlan St FK5 13 B4
McLaren Ave EH49 55 B4
McLaren Ct FK5 13 C4
MacLaren Terr FK2 14 C4
McNab Gdns FK1 40 A4
Macpherson Pl 6 FK1 40 A4
McTaggart Ave FK6 10 A4
McVean Pl FK4 24 B2
Madderfield Mews EH49 48 C1
MADDISTON 53 C4
Maddiston Prim Sch FK2 53 A4
Maddiston Rd FK2 43 C2
Madill Pl FK5 6 B1
Maggie Wood's Loan
Falkirk FK1 29 C2
Falkirk FK1 29 C3
Magnus Rd EH51 35 A3
MAIDENPARK 37 B4
Maidenpark Pl EH51 37 B4
Maidlands EH49 49 A1
Main Rd FK3 19 A2
Mains Rd EH49 56 C4
Main St
Bo'ness EH51 21 B2
Bonnybridge FK4 26 B3
California FK1 51 A3
Falkirk, Bainsford FK2 15 A1
Falkirk, Camelon FK1 29 B3

Main St *continued*
Falkirk, Carronshore FK2 7 B1
Grangemouth, Brightons FK2 43 B2
Grangemouth, Rumford FK2 44 A1
Linlithgow EH49 47 B1
Polmont FK2 43 C4
Redding FK2 43 A4
Shieldhill FK1 50 B4
Stenhousemuir FK5 14 A4
Stenhousemuir, Larbert FK5 13 B4
Majors Loan FK1 30 A2
Majors Pl FK1 30 A1
Malcolm Dr FK5 6 A2
Maltings The EH49 56 B4
Mamre Dr FK1 51 A3
Mandela Ave FK2 15 B1
Mannfield Ave FK4 25 C2
Manor St FK1 30 B2
Manor Wynd FK2 53 B3
Man O' War Way EH51 21 C2
Manse Pl FK1 30 B2
Manse Rd EH49 57 B4
Mansionhouse Rd FK1 29 A3
Manuel Rigg FK2 52 C4
Manuel Terr EH49 55 A4
Maple Ave FK5 6 B1
Maple Pl FK6 2 B1
Maranatha Cres FK2 43 A2
Marchlands Ave EH51 21 B1
Marchlands La EH51 21 B1
Marchlands Terr EH51 21 A1
Marchmont Ave FK2 43 C4
Marchmont Ct FK2 44 A4
Marchmont Mews FK2 44 A4
Margaret Ave FK4 24 A1
Margaret Ct FK6 10 A3
Margaret Dr FK4 26 A4
Margaret Terr FK5 6 A2
Mariner Ave FK1 28 B3
Mariner Dr FK1 28 B3
Mariner Gdns FK1 28 C4
Mariner Rd FK1 28 C3
Mariner St FK1 28 B3
Market La EH49 48 B1
Market St EH51 21 A2
Marmion Rd FK3 33 A3
Marmion St FK2 15 A2
Marshall St FK3 17 C2
Marshall Terr FK3 17 C2
Marshall Twr FK1 31 A2
Maryfield Dr EH51 39 A4
Maryfield Pl FK1 28 B2
Maryflats Pl FK3 18 A1
Mary Sq FK2 32 A2
Mary St FK2 31 C2
Mary Street Rdbt FK2 31 C1
Mather Terr FK2 31 C2
Mathew Ct FK3 17 C2
Mavisbank Ave FK1 50 A4
Maxwell Twr FK1 31 A1
Mayfield Dr FK4 24 B1
Mayfield Mews 2 FK1 29 C2
Mayfield Rd FK2 43 A4

Meadowbank St FK2 43 A3
Meadow Ct FK6 2 C2
Meadow St FK1 30 C2
Meadows The
Falkirk, Carronshore FK2 15 A4
Falkirk FK1 30 C2
Meeks Rd FK2 30 B3
Melrose Dr FK3 33 C4
Melrose Pl 9 FK1 30 B2
Melville La 3 FK1 30 B3
Melville St 2 FK1 30 B3
Merchiston Ave FK2 14 C1
Merchiston Gdns FK2 30 A4
Merchiston Ind Est FK2 15 B2
Merchiston Rd FK2 30 A4
Merchiston Rdbt FK2 30 A4
Merchiston Terr FK2 14 C1
Meredith Dr FK5 6 B1
Merker Terr EH49 56 C4
Merkland Dr FK1 41 C3
Merrick Rd FK3 33 C3
Merrick Way FK3 33 C3
Merville Cres FK1 51 A3
Merville Terr FK1 51 A3
MIDDLEFIELD 31 A4
Middlefield Ind Est FK2 15 C1
Middlefield Rd FK2 31 A4
Middlemass Ct FK2 30 B4
Middle Street La FK3 17 B3
Midthorn Cres FK2 31 B3
Millar Pl
Bonnybridge FK4 26 B1
Falkirk FK2 6 C3
Millbank Terr 4 FK2 44 A1
Millburn St FK2 31 A3
Mill Ct FK2 7 A1
Miller Cres EH51 39 A3
Millerfield EH49 47 B1
Miller Pk FK2 44 A3
Miller Rd EH51 35 B3
Millfield Dr FK2 43 C4
Millflats St FK2 14 C3
Millhall Gdns FK2 33 C1
Mill Lade EH49 47 C1
Mill Rd
Falkirk FK2 7 A1
Linlithgow EH49 47 A1
Mill Road Ind Est EH49 47 B2
Milnquarter Rd FK4 26 A1
Milton Cl FK6 2 C1
Milton Pl FK6 2 C1
Milton Row FK6 3 A1
MINGLE 38 A4
Mingle Pl EH51 38 A4
Mission La 8 FK1 30 B2
Moffat Ave FK2 7 B1
Moncks Rd FK1 31 A2
Montfort Pl FK1 30 B1
Montgomery Cres FK2 15 A4
Montgomery Dr FK2 15 A4
Montgomery Pl FK2 15 A4

Montgomery St
Falkirk FK2 31 B3
Grangemouth FK3 32 C4
Montgomery Well FK2 15 A4
Montrose Rd FK2 44 B3
Montrose Way FK4 25 A3
Morar Ct FK3 33 A3
Morar Dr FK2 15 B3
Morar Pl FK3 33 A3
Moray Dr EH49 56 C4
Moray Pl
Grangemouth FK3 18 A1
Linlithgow EH49 56 C4
Moray Prim Sch FK3 18 A1
Moriston Ct FK3 33 B2
Morrison Ave FK4 25 C4
Morven Ct FK1 41 A4
Morven Dr FK2 43 B4
Mossgiel St FK1 28 B3
Mossgiel Terr FK2 32 A1
Mount Bartholomew FK4 26 A3
Mountbatten St FK3 32 C3
Moy Ct FK3 33 A3
Mudale Ct FK1 41 B3
Muiravonside Ctry Pk★ EH49 54 C2
Muirdyke Ave FK2 7 B1
Muirend Ct EH51 38 B4
Muirepark Ct EH51 38 A4
Muirfield Rd FK5 14 A4
Muirhall Pl FK5 5 B1
Muirhall Rd FK5 5 B1
Muirhead Ave FK2 14 C2
Muirhead Rd FK5 6 A2
MUIRHOUSES 39 A3
Muirhouses Ave EH51 38 C4
Muirhouses Cres EH51 38 C4
Muirhouses Sq EH51 22 A1
Muirpark Dr FK1 50 B4
Muir St FK5 13 C4
Mull Ct FK3 33 A4
Mulloch Ave 1 FK2 14 C2
Mumrills Rd FK2 32 C2
MUNGAL 14 C2
Mungalend FK2 15 A1
Mungalend Ct FK2 15 A1
Mungalend Rdbt FK2 15 A1
Mungalhead Rd FK2 14 C1
Mungal Pl FK2 15 A2
Munro Gdns FK2 31 C1
Munro St FK5 6 A1
Murnin Rd FK4 26 A2
Murnin Road Ind Est FK4 26 A2
Murray Cres FK2 53 B4
Mylne Pl FK2 15 A4
Myothill Rd FK6 9 C1
Myreton Rd FK3 33 A4
Myreton Way FK1 29 C1

N

Nailer Rd FK1 29 B4
Nairn Ct FK1 41 B3
Naismith Ct FK3 18 A3
Namayo Ave FK2 32 A2
Napier Cres FK2 14 C1
Napier Pl FK2 14 C1
Neidpath Dr FK5 6 C2
Neilson St FK1 30 B2
Nelson Gdns FK3 18 A3
Nelson Rd EH51 35 B4
Nelson St FK3 18 A2
Netherfaulds Dr FK6 9 C3
Netherfield Rd FK2 43 B3
Nethermains Prim Sch FK6 9 C3
Nethermains Rd FK6 9 B4
Nevis Pl
Falkirk FK1 41 A4
Grangemouth FK3 33 B3
Newbiggin Rd FK3 33 B4
Newcarron Ct 3 FK2 14 C2
New Carron Rd FK2, FK5 6 C1
New Hallglen Rd FK1 41 B4
Newhouse Bsns Pk FK3 17 B1
Newhouse Rd FK3 17 C1
Newlands Rd
Grangemouth FK3 32 C4
Polmont FK2 43 A2
Newlands Road Rdbt 5 FK2 43 A2
Newmarket Ctr 5 FK1 30 B3
Newmarket St 7 FK1 30 B3
Newton Ave FK2 8 C1
Newton Rd FK2 16 C4
NEWTOWN 37 C4
Newtown EH51 37 C4
Newtown Cotts EH51 37 C4
Newtown St EH51 37 C4
New Well Wynd EH49 57 A4
Nicholson Pl FK1 40 A4
Nicolton Ave FK2 43 C1
Nicolton Ct 2 FK2 44 A1
Nicolton Rd FK2 44 C2
Ninian Rd EH51 35 B4
Nisbet Dr FK6 9 C4
Nobel View FK2 42 B2
North Ave FK2 44 C1
Northbank Ct EH51 38 A3
Northbank Dr EH51 38 A3
Northbank Pk EH51 37 C3
North Bridge St FK3 17 B3
NORTH BROOMAGE 4 C2
North Broomage Rdbt FK5 4 C1
Northfield Rd FK6 2 B2
North Main St FK2 7 B1
North Shore Rd FK3 18 A4
North St
Bo'ness EH51 21 A2
Falkirk FK2 15 A2
Norwood Ave FK4 11 A1
Norwood Ct FK4 11 A1
Norwood Pl FK4 11 A1
Nursery Rd FK1 29 B2

O

Oakbank FK2 42 B4
Oak Dr FK5 13 C3
Oakhill View FK2 53 C4
Oakwood Education Trust FK2 31 C2
Oatlands Pk EH49 57 C3

Ochil Dr
Maddiston FK2 . . . . . . 53 B3
Stenhousemuir FK5 . . . . 6 A1
Ochil St FK3 . . . . 17 C1
Ochil Terr FK2 . . . . . . 14 C4
Ochiltree Terr
FK1 . . . . 28 B3
Ochil View
Denny FK6 . . . . 9 C2
Shieldhill FK1 . . . . 41 B1
Ochil View Ct FK5 . . . . 5 B3
Ochilview Pk (Stenhousemuir FC) FK5 . . . . 5 C1
Ochilview Pl
EH51 . . . . 37 B4
Ochilview Rd
EH51 . . . . 37 B4
Ochilview Terr
EH51 . . . . 37 B4
Old Bellsdyke Rd
FK5 . . . . 4 C1
Old Denny Rd FK5 . . . . 4 C1
Old Redding Rd
FK2 . . . . 31 C1
Old Refinery Rd
FK3 . . . . 18 C2
Old St Mary's La
EH51 . . . . 21 B2
Oldwalls Pl FK3 . . . . . 18 A1
Oldwalls Rd FK3, EH51 . . . . 19 B2
Oliver Rd FK1 . . . . 31 A2
Orchard Gr FK2 . . . . . 44 A4
Orchard Rd FK3 . . . . . 19 B2
Orchard St
Falkirk FK1 . . . . 30 B3
Grangemouth FK3 . . . . 17 C1
Orchard The FK2 . . . . 43 B2
Orkney Pl FK1 . . . . . . 40 C4
Ormond Ct FK5 . . . . . . 4 C1
Oronsay Ave
Maddiston FK2 . . . . . . 53 A4
Maddiston FK2 . . . . . . 53 B4
Osborne Gdns
FK1 . . . . 29 C1
Osborne St FK1 . . . . . 29 C1
Oswald Ave FK3 . . . . . 18 B2
Oswald St FK1 . . . . . . 30 B2
Overton Cres
Denny FK6 . . . . 9 C3
Redding FK2 . . . . 42 C3
Overton Rd
Grangemouth, Bowhouse FK3 . . . . . . 33 B4
Grangemouth, Oil Refinery FK3 . . . . 19 A2
Overton Terr FK6 . . . . . 9 B4
Oxgang Rd FK3 . . . . . 18 A1

P

Palmer Ct FK3 . . . . . . 17 C2
Panbrae Rd EH51 . . . 20 C1
Panstead St FK3 . . . . 18 A1
Pardovan Pl FK1 . . . . 29 C4
Paris Ave FK6 . . . . 10 A3
Paris St FK3 . . . . 18 A2
Park Ave
Denny FK4 . . . . 25 B4
Grangemouth FK2 . . . . 43 B2
Laurieston FK2 . . . . . . 31 C2
Stenhousemuir FK5 . . . . 13 C3
Park Cres
Falkirk FK2 . . . . 14 C4
Westquarter FK2 . . . . . 32 A1
Park Dr
Grangemouth FK2 . . . . 43 B2
Stenhousemuir FK5 . . . . 13 C4
Parkend Cres
FK1 . . . . 50 A4
PARKFOOT 24 C2
Parkfoot Ct FK1 . . . . . 30 B1
Park Gdns 4 FK2 . . . 43 B2
Parkhall Dr FK2 . . . . . 53 B4
Parkhead Rd
Falkirk FK1 . . . . 40 C3
Linlithgow EH49 . . . . . 48 A2
Parkhead Smallholdings
EH49 . . . . 48 B3
Park La EH51 . . . . 21 C1
Park Rd
Falkirk FK2 . . . . 14 C3
Grangemouth FK3 . . . . 17 C2
Park St
Bonnybridge FK4 . . . . 26 C2
Falkirk FK1 . . . . 30 B3
Park Terr FK2 . . . . 43 B2
Park View FK2 . . . . . . 43 C2
Parkview Ave
FK1 . . . . 40 A4
Park View Ct FK1 . . . . 29 B3
Paterson Dr FK1 . . . . 50 A4
Paterson Pl FK4 . . . . 26 C3
Paterson Twr
FK1 . . . . 31 A2
Patrick Dr FK1 . . . . . . 41 C1
Pearson Ave FK4 . . . . 25 A3
Pearson Pl FK4 . . . . . 25 A3
Peathill Rd FK4 . . . . . 26 A4
Peathill Terr FK4 . . . . 26 A3
Peddie Pl FK3 . . . . . . 18 A2
Pembroke St FK5 . . . . 5 B1
Pender Gdns FK2 . . . 43 C1
Penders La FK1 . . . . . 30 A3
Pennelton Pl
EH51 . . . . 37 B3
Pentland Way
FK3 . . . . 33 B3
Philip Ave EH49 . . . . . 47 C1
Philip Dr FK5 . . . . 13 C4
Philip St FK2 . . . . 15 A1
Philpingstone La
EH51 . . . . 22 A1
Philpingstone Rd
EH51 . . . . 22 A1
Pier Rd EH51 . . . . 22 A2
Pilgrims Hill
EH49 . . . . 49 B2
Pine Gn EH51 . . . . 37 A2
Pine Gr FK2 . . . . 42 C4
Pine Wlk FK5 . . . . 13 C3
Pirleyhill Dr FK1 . . . . 50 B4
Pirleyhill Gdns
FK1 . . . . 40 B4
Pleasance FK1 . . . . . . 30 B2
Pleasance Ct 12
FK2 . . . . 30 B2
Pleasance Gdns
FK1 . . . . 30 B2
Pleasance Rd
FK1 . . . . 30 B1
Pleasance Sq 11
FK1 . . . . 30 B2
POLMONT 44 A4
Polmont House Gdns
FK2 . . . . 43 C3
Polmont Pk FK2 . . . . 33 B1
Polmont Rd FK2 . . . . 32 B1
Polmont Sta FK2 . . . . 43 C3
POLMONT STATION 43 C3
Polwarth Ave
FK2 . . . . 43 A2
Poolewe Dr FK2 . . . . 43 A4
Poplar St FK3 . . . . 17 B1
Portal Rd FK3 . . . . 32 C3
Port Downie FK1 . . . . 29 A3
Portree Cres FK2 . . . . 44 B3
Potter Pl FK2 . . . . 8 B1
Powdrake Rd FK3 . . . 18 B2
Preston Ave EH49 . . . 57 A4
Preston Cres
EH49 . . . . 57 A4
Preston Ct EH49 . . . . 57 A4
Preston House Gdns
EH49 . . . . 56 C2
Preston Pk EH49 . . . . 57 A4
Preston Rd EH49 . . . . 57 A4
Preston Terr
EH49 . . . . 57 A4
Pretoria Pl FK2 . . . . . 43 C3
Pretoria Rd FK5 . . . . . 13 A3
Primrose Ave
FK3 . . . . 32 B4
Primrose Avenue Ind Est FK3 . . . . 32 B4
Primrose St FK4 . . . . 26 B4
Princess St FK4 . . . . . 26 B3
Princes St
California FK1 . . . . 51 A3
Falkirk FK1 . . . . 30 B3
Grangemouth FK3 . . . . 18 A2
Priory Pl EH49 . . . . . . 46 A1
Priory Rd
Linlithgow EH49 . . . . . 57 A3
Whitecross EH49 . . . . . 55 A4
Prospecthill Rd
FK1 . . . . 40 B4
Prospect St FK1 . . . . . 29 C3
Providence Brae
EH51 . . . . 21 A2
Provost Rd
Bo'ness EH51 . . . . 36 C4
Linlithgow EH49 . . . . . 48 C1

Q

Quarrolhall Cres
FK2 . . . . 7 A1
Quarry Brae FK2 . . . . 43 C2
Quarryknowes The
EH51 . . . . 37 B4
Queen's Cres FK1 . . . 29 C3
Queens Ct FK5 . . . . 5 C1
Queens Dr
Denny FK6 . . . . 3 A1
Falkirk FK1 . . . . 29 C3
Stenhousemuir FK5 . . . . 5 B1
Queen's Dr
California FK1 . . . . 51 A3
Stenhousemuir FK5 . . . . 13 B4
Queen St
Falkirk FK2 . . . . 30 C3
Grangemouth FK3 . . . . 18 B2
Quench Rd FK3 . . . . . 34 B3

R

Rae Ct FK2 . . . . 7 B1
Rae St FK5 . . . . 5 C1
Rainhill Ave FK2 . . . . 52 C4
Rainhill Ct 1
FK2 . . . . 44 A1
Raleigh Ct FK1 . . . . . . 29 B3
Ramsay Ave FK2 . . . . 32 A1
Randolph Cres
FK2 . . . . 43 B2
Randolph Gdns
FK6 . . . . 9 C3
Randyford Rd
FK2 . . . . 31 A3
Randyford St FK2 . . . 31 B3
Range Rd EH51 . . . . . 19 C2
Rankin Cres FK4 . . . . 25 A3
Rannoch Pl
Shieldhill FK1 . . . . 41 C1
Stenhousemuir FK5 . . . . 6 B2
Rannoch Rd FK3 . . . . 33 A2
Rattray St EH51 . . . . . 21 C2
Redbrae Ave
EH51 . . . . 38 A3
Redbrae Rd FK1 . . . . 29 A4
REDDING 43 A3
Redding Ind Est
FK2 . . . . 42 B3
REDDINGMUIRHEAD 42 B2
Redding Rd
Grangemouth FK2 . . . . 43 B2
Laurieston FK2 . . . . . . 42 A4
Redding FK2 . . . . 42 C3
Redding Road Rdbt
FK2 . . . . 42 A4
Reddoch Rd
Grangemouth FK2 . . . . 34 A2
Grangemouth FK3 . . . . 33 C3
Redhouse Ind Est
FK2 . . . . 42 C2
Redpath Dr FK2 . . . . . . 6 C2
Reedlands Dr FK6 . . . . 9 C1
Regent Sq EH49 . . . . . 48 C1
Register St EH51 . . . . 21 A2
Reilly Gdns FK4 . . . . . 26 B1
Reilly Rd FK4 . . . . 26 B1
Rennie St FK1 . . . . . . 30 A1
Reynard Gdns
EH49 . . . . 55 B4
Riccarton Rd
EH49 . . . . 57 A3
Richmond Dr FK2 . . . 43 A2
Richmond Terr
EH51 . . . . 21 A1
Rifle Rd EH51 . . . . 19 C2
Ritchie Pl
Bo'ness EH51 . . . . 38 A3
Grangemouth FK3 . . . . 32 C3
Rivaldsgreen Cres
EH49 . . . . 57 B4
Riverside Ct EH49 . . . 47 A1
Riverside Rd FK3 . . . . 34 B3
River St FK2 . . . . 14 C3
Road 4a FK3 . . . . 34 C4
Road 4b FK3 . . . . 34 C4
Road 5a FK3 . . . . 19 B1
Road 30b FK3 . . . . 34 B4
Road 30c FK3 . . . . 34 B4
Road 4 FK3 . . . . 34 C4
Road 6 FK3 . . . . 34 C4
Road 7 FK3 . . . . 19 B1
Road 8 FK3 . . . . 19 B1
Road 9 FK3 . . . . 19 B1
Road 10 FK3 . . . . 19 B1
Road 11 FK3 . . . . 34 C4
Road 13 FK3 . . . . 34 C4
Road 15 FK3 . . . . 34 C4
Road 17 FK3 . . . . 34 A4
Road 21 FK3 . . . . 34 A4
Road 24 FK3 . . . . 34 A4
Road 25 FK3 . . . . 34 B4
Road 27 FK3 . . . . 34 B4
Road 28 FK3 . . . . 34 B4
Road 29 FK3 . . . . 34 B4
Road 31 FK3 . . . . 34 B4
Road 32 FK3 . . . . 34 B4
Road 33 FK2, FK3 . . . . 34 B3
Robert Bruce Ct
FK5 . . . . 12 C4
Robert Hardie Ct
FK5 . . . . 13 B4
Robert Kay Pl FK5 . . . . 5 B3
Roberts Ave FK2 . . . . 43 B4
Robertson Ave
FK4 . . . . 26 B4
Robertson Ct FK5 . . . 13 C4
Rockville Gr EH49 . . . 57 B4
Rodel Dr FK2 . . . . 44 A3
Rodgers St FK6 . . . . . 10 A3
Rodney St FK3 . . . . . . 32 C4
Roebuck Pl EH51 . . . . 37 A3
Roman Bldgs FK2 . . . 29 A3
Roman Dr FK1 . . . . . . 29 A3
Roman Rd FK4 . . . . . . 26 A2
Roman Way EH51 . . . . 37 A3
Ronades Rd FK2 . . . . 14 C2
Ronald Cres FK5 . . . . 13 A3
Ronaldshay Cres
FK3 . . . . 18 A2
ROSEBANK 2 C2
Rosebank Ave
FK1 . . . . 29 C3
Rosebank Gdns
FK2 . . . . 42 C1
Rosebank Pl FK1 . . . . 29 C3
Rosebank Rdbt
FK1 . . . . 29 C3
Rosehall Terr
FK1 . . . . 30 B2
Roselea Dr FK2 . . . . . 43 C2
Rosemary Ct FK6 . . . . . 9 C4
Rosemead Terr
FK1 . . . . 51 A3
Rosemount Gdns
FK1 . . . . 50 B4
Rose St FK4 . . . . 26 B4
Rose Terr
Denny FK6 . . . . 9 C3
Stenhousemuir FK5 . . . . 6 B1
Ross Cres FK1 . . . . . . 28 C3
Roughlands Cres
FK2 . . . . 7 A1
Roughlands Dr
FK2 . . . . 6 C1
Roundel The FK2 . . . . 15 C1
Rowan Cres FK1 . . . . 28 A2
Rowantree Wlk
FK5 . . . . 5 A2
Roxburgh Pl FK5 . . . . . 6 B2
Roxburgh St FK3 . . . . 18 B2
Royal Scottish National Hospl The
FK5 . . . . 4 B1
Royal Terr EH49 . . . . . 57 A4
Rulley View FK6 . . . . . . 2 B2
RUMFORD 43 C1
Run The EH51 . . . . 22 A1
Russell Hill Ct
FK5 . . . . 13 A3
Russell Pl FK4 . . . . . . 25 A3
Russel St FK2 . . . . 30 B4

S

Sacred Heart RC Prim Sch FK3 . . . . . . 33 B4
Sainford Cres
FK2 . . . . 14 C3
St Andrew's Ct
FK5 . . . . 5 A1
St Andrews Pl 10
FK1 . . . . 30 B2
St Andrew's RC Prim Sch FK1 . . . . 31 B2
St Catherine FK2 . . . . 44 A1
St Crispin's Pl
FK1 . . . . 30 B2
St David's Ct FK5 . . . 13 A3
St Francis Xavier's RC Prim Sch
FK2 . . . . 30 A4
St George's Ct
FK5 . . . . 13 A3
St Giles Sq FK1 . . . . . 28 B4
St Giles Way FK1 . . . . 28 B4
St John's Ave
Falkirk FK2 . . . . 30 C4
Linlithgow EH49 . . . . . 57 A4
St John's Ct FK2 . . . . 30 C4
St John's Gate FK6 . . . 9 B4
St John's Gdns
FK6 . . . . 9 B4
St John's Gr FK6 . . . . . 9 B4
St John's Way
EH51 . . . . 37 C3
St Joseph's RC Prim Sch
Bonnybridge FK4 . . . . 26 B2
Linlithgow EH49 . . . . . 57 A4
St Magdalenes
EH49 . . . . 48 C1
St Margaret's Cres
FK2 . . . . 43 C4
St Margarets Gdns
FK2 . . . . 43 B4
St Margaret's Prim Sch FK2 . . . . 43 B3
St Marys Pl FK3 . . . . . 18 A2
St Mary's RC Prim Sch EH51 . . . . 21 B1
St Michaels La
EH49 . . . . 48 C1
St Michael's Wynd
EH49 . . . . 48 B1

St Modans Ct 13 FK1 30 B2
St Mungo's High Sch FK2 30 A4
St Ninian's Ave EH49 47 C2
St Ninian's Rd EH49 48 A1
St Ninian's Way EH49 48 A1
St Patrick's RC Prim Sch FK6 3 A1
Salmon Inn Pk FK2 43 A4
Salmon Inn Rd FK2 43 B4
Saltcoats Dr FK3 18 A1
Saltcoats Rd FK3 19 A2
Sandyford Ave EH49 55 B4
Sandyloan FK2 32 B2
Sandyloan Cres FK2 32 B1
Sawers Ave FK6 9 C3
School Brae EH51 21 A2
School Rd
Laurieston FK2 32 A1
Redding FK2 42 C4
School View
Bo'ness EH51 21 B1
Redding FK2 43 A3
School Wlk FK5 5 C1
Sclandersburn Rd FK6 9 B2
Scotia Pl FK2 30 C3
Scotlands Cl EH51 21 A2
Scott Ave FK2 43 C4
Scottish Prison Service Coll FK2 43 A2
Scottish Railway Exhibition★ EH51 21 B2
Scott St FK3 33 A3
Scott Terr FK2 15 A3
Seabegs Cres FK4 26 A2
Seabegs Pl FK4 25 C2
Seabegs Rd FK4 25 C2
Seabegs Wood Antonine Wall★ FK4 25 B1
Seafield Ct 3 FK1 40 A4
Seaforth Rd FK2 15 B3
Sealock Ct FK3 33 A3
Seaton Pl FK1 31 A2
Seaview Pl EH51 21 A2
Seaview Terr FK2 53 A4
Second St
Grangemouth, Chemical Works FK3 35 A4
Grangemouth, Oil Refinery FK3 18 C2
Seton Terr EH51 21 C1
Seventh St
Grangemouth, Chemical Works EH51 35 B3
Grangemouth, Oil Refinery FK3 19 B2
Shafto Pl EH51 37 C3
Shanks Ave FK6 10 A2
Shannon Dr FK1 29 C2
Sharp Terr FK3 32 C4
Shaw Pl FK3 32 C3
Sheriffs Pk EH49 49 C2
Sherriff La FK5 6 B1
Shiel Ct FK3 33 A2
SHIELDHILL 50 B4
Shieldhill Prim Sch FK1 50 B4
Shieldhill Rd FK2 42 B2
Shiel Gdns FK2 15 B3
Sidlaw Pl FK3 33 B3
Silk Ho 1 FK1 30 B3
Silverdale Rd FK2 43 C2
Simpson Dr FK2 53 B4
Simpson St FK1 29 B4
Sinclair Cres FK6 9 C3
Sinclair Pl FK2 14 C3
Sir John Graham Ct FK5 13 A3
Sir William Wallace Ct FK5 5 A1
Sixth St
Grangemouth, Chemical Works EH51 35 B4
Grangemouth, Oil Refinery FK3 19 A2
Skaithmuir Ave FK2 7 A1
Skaithmuir Cres FK2 7 A1
Skelmorlie Pl FK5 6 B2
Skene St FK4 26 A4
SKINFLATS 8 B1
Skye Ct FK3 33 A4
Skye Dr FK2 44 A3
Slamannan Rd FK1 40 B4
Smallburn Pl FK3 33 B4
Smiddy Brae FK2 33 C2
Smith Pl FK6 9 C3
Smith St FK2 15 A1
Snab Brae EH51 37 A4
Snab La EH51 20 B1
Solway Dr FK6 9 C1
Souillac Dr FK6 9 B3
Souter Way FK5 5 B2
South Ave FK2 44 C1
South Bantaskine Dr FK1 30 A1
South Bantaskine Rd FK1 30 A1
South Brae FK2 53 B3
South Bridge St FK3 17 B3
SOUTH BROOMAGE 13 C3
South Broomage Ave FK5 13 B3
South Craigs Rd FK2 43 C1
South Lumley St FK3 17 C2
South Marshall St FK3 17 C1
South Melville La 4 FK1 30 B3
South Philpingstone La EH51 22 A1
South Pleasance Ave FK1 30 B2
South Rd FK3 34 B3
South Shore Rd FK3 19 A4
South St EH51 21 A2
South View FK5 13 C3
Spence St FK4 26 A4
Spey Ct FK3 33 A3
Spinkhill FK2 42 A4
Springbank Gdns FK2 30 C3
Springfield Ct EH49 49 B2
Springfield Dr FK1 29 C3
Springfield Prim Sch EH49 49 B2
Springfield Rd
Denny FK6 10 B4
Linlithgow EH49 49 A1
Staffa Pl FK1 40 C4
Standrigg Ave FK2 43 A1
Standrigg Gdns FK2 43 B1
Standrigg Rd FK2 51 C4
Stanley Gdns FK2 53 A4
Stark Ave FK1 29 A3
Stark's Brae EH51 21 B1
Station Rd
Brightons FK2 43 C3
Grangemouth FK3 17 C3
Linlithgow EH49 48 B1
Longcroft FK4 24 B2
Whitecross EH49 55 A4
Steadings The EH49 46 C2
Steel Cres FK6 10 B3
STENHOUSEMUIR 5 C1
Stenhousemuir Prim Sch FK5 5 C1
Stenhouse Rd FK2 14 B4
Stephens Croft FK2 14 B2
Steps St FK5 6 A1
Stevenson Ave FK2 43 B3
Stevenson Ct FK2 15 A3
Stevenson St FK3 33 A3
Stewart Ave
Bo'ness EH51 21 A2
Linlithgow EH49 56 C4
Stenhousemuir FK2 14 C4
Stewart Rd FK2 30 C3
Stewart St FK4 25 C3
Stirling Rd
Larbert, North Broomage FK5 4 C1
Larbert, South Broomage FK2, FK5 13 B2
Torwood FK5 4 A3
Stirling St
Denny, Dunipace FK6 2 C2
Denny FK6 10 A4
STONEYWOOD 9 B4
Stoneywood Pk FK6 9 A4
Strachan Ct EH51 20 B1
Strachan St FK1 29 B2
Strang's Pl FK1 51 A3
Strathearn Ct FK3 18 A2
Strathmiglo Pl FK5 6 B2
Strawberry Bank EH49 57 B4
Striven Dr FK2 15 B3
Strowan Rd FK3 18 B1
Strowan Sq FK3 18 B1
Stuart Gr FK3 32 B4
Styles Pl FK1 40 A4
Suilven Hts FK2 32 A1
SUMMERFORD 29 A2
Summerford FK1 29 A2
Summerford Gdns FK1 29 A2
Summerford Rd FK1 29 A2
Sunart Pl FK3 33 A3
Sunnybrae Terr FK2 53 A4
Sunnylaw Pl FK1 29 C1
Sunnyside Ave FK2 43 A1
Sunnyside Cotts FK2 43 B1
Sunnyside Ct FK2 43 A2
Sunnyside Dr FK2 43 A1
Sunnyside Rd
Falkirk FK1 29 C3
Grangemouth FK2 43 B1
Sunnyside St FK1 29 B4
Sutherland Dr FK6 9 C2
Sutton Park Cres FK5 6 A1
Sutton Pl FK2 31 A3
Swan Pl FK3 33 A3
Sword's Way FK2 14 C3
Sycamore Ave EH51 37 A3
Sylvan Gr EH51 36 C3
Symington Pl FK2 7 A1
Symon Twr FK1 31 A2

T

Tait Dr FK5 13 B2
Talbot St FK3 17 C2
Talman Gdns FK2 33 B1
TAMFOURHILL 28 C2
Tamfourhill Ave FK1 28 C2
Tamfourhill Ind Est FK1 28 C2
Tamfourhill Rd FK1 28 C2
Tanera Ct FK1 40 C4
Tanners Rd FK1 30 A2
Tantallon Dr FK2 6 C1
Tappoch Pl FK5 4 C1
Taransay Dr FK2 44 A3
Tarbert Pl FK2 44 A3
Tarduff Dr FK2 53 B3
Tarduff Pl FK6 9 A4
Target Rd FK3 19 B2
Taylor Ct
Falkirk FK2 15 B1
Grangemouth FK3 18 A3
Taylor's Rd FK5 13 B3
Taymouth Rd FK2 44 B3
Tay St
Falkirk FK2 15 B3
Grangemouth FK3 16 C3
Tedder St FK3 32 C3
Telford Pl EH49 47 A1
Telford Sq FK1 29 B4
Telford View EH49 56 A4
Temple Denny Rd FK6 9 C4
Tenacres Pl FK3 33 B4
Tenacres Rd FK3 19 A1
Teviot St FK1 29 C2
Third St
Grangemouth, Chemical Works EH51 35 A4
Grangemouth, Oil Refinery FK3 18 C2
Thirlestane EH51 21 C2
Thirlestane Pl EH51 21 C2
Thistle Ave
Denny FK6 2 C1
Grangemouth FK3 32 B3
Thistle St FK2 30 C4
Thomson Cres FK1 29 B1
Thornbridge Gdns FK2 31 B2
Thornbridge Rd FK2 31 B3
Thornbridge Sq FK2 31 B3
Thorndene Ct 2 FK1 40 A4
Thornhill Ct FK2 30 C4
Thornhill Rd FK2 30 C4
Thornton Ave FK4 26 B4
Thornton Gdns FK4 26 B4
Three Bridges Rdbt FK1 28 A4
Thrums The FK2 32 A2
Timmons Pl FK6 9 C3
Tinto Dr FK3 33 B3
Tipperary Pl FK5 14 A4
Tiree Cres FK2 43 B4
Tiree Pl FK1 40 C3
Tolbooth St 3 FK1 30 B2
Tolsta Cres FK2 44 A3
Tophill Entry FK1 29 C3
Toravon Dr FK2 53 B4
Torlea Pl FK5 5 A1
Torosay Ave FK2 53 A4
Torridon Ave FK2 15 B3
TORWOOD 4 A4
Torwood Ave
Grangemouth FK3 33 B4
Larbert FK5 13 A4
Torwood Sch FK5 4 A4
Tower Gdns The EH51 22 A1
Towers Ct FK2 30 B4
Town House St FK6 10 A4
Troup Ct FK3 17 C2
Tryst Pk FK5 5 B3
Tryst Rd FK5 5 C1
Tudor Ct FK2 43 A4
Tulliallan Pl FK5 6 C2
Tummel Pl
Grangemouth FK3 33 B2
Stenhousemuir FK5 6 A1
Turret Dr FK2 44 B4
Turret Rd FK3 33 A3
Twain Ave FK5 6 C1
Tweed St FK3 16 C3
Tygetshaugh Ct FK6 2 C2

U

Union Ct EH51 21 B2
Union Gdns FK1 29 A3
Union Pl
Brightons FK2 43 B3
Larbert FK5 13 A3
Union Rd
Falkirk FK1 29 A3
Grangemouth FK3 17 C3
Linlithgow EH49 57 A4
Union St
Bo'ness EH51 21 A2
Bo'ness EH51 21 B2
Falkirk FK2 15 A1
Stenhousemuir FK5 6 A1
Universal Rd FK2 16 A1
Upper Newmarket St 6 FK1 30 B3
Ure Cres FK4 26 A4
Ure Ct FK3 17 C2

V

Vale Of Bonny View FK4 25 C3
Vale Pl FK6 3 A1
Valeview FK5 13 C4
Valleyview Dr FK2 14 C2
Valleyview Pl FK2 14 C1
Vellore Rd FK2 53 B4
Vennel The
Denny FK6 10 A4
Linlithgow EH49 48 B1
Vicar St FK1 30 B3
Victoria Mills Ind Est EH51 22 A2
Victoria Pl
Bo'ness EH51 21 C1
Brightons FK2 43 B3
Victoria Prim Sch FK2 31 A4
Victoria Rd
Falkirk FK2 30 C4
Grangemouth FK3 18 A2
Larbert FK5 13 A3
Viewfield Rd FK4 23 A1
Viewforth EH51 21 B1
Viewforth Dr FK2 32 B2
Villabank FK6 10 A4
Vorlich Dr FK1 41 C1

W

Waddell St FK2 . . . . . 15 B4
Waggon Rd
Bo'ness EH51 . . . . 21 A2
Falkirk FK2 . . . . 15 A1
Grangemouth FK2 . . . . 43 A2
Waldie Ave EH49 . . . . 57 B3
Walker Dr FK4 . . . . . . 25 A3
Wallace Bldgs
FK2 . . . . 30 B4
Wallace Brae Ave
FK2 . . . . 43 A2
Wallace Brae Bank
FK2 . . . . 43 A2
Wallace Brae Ct 1
FK2 . . . . 43 A2
Wallace Brae Dr
FK2 . . . . 43 A2
Wallace Brae Gdns
4 FK2. . . . . 43 A2
Wallace Brae Gr 2
FK2 . . . . 43 A2
Wallace Brae Pl 3
FK2 . . . . 43 A2
Wallace Brae Rise
FK2 . . . . 43 A2
Wallace Cres
Denny FK6. . . . . 9 B4
Grangemouth FK2. . . . 43 B2
Wallace Ct FK3 . . . . . 17 C2
Wallacelea FK2 . . . . . 43 C1
Wallace Pl FK2. . . . . . 30 C4
Wallace St
Falkirk FK2 . . . . 30 C4
Grangemouth FK3. . . . 17 C2
WALLACESTONE . . . 42 C1
Wallacestone Brae
FK2 . . . . 42 C1
Wallacestone Prim Sch FK2 . . . . 43 B1
Wallace View
Bo'ness EH51 . . . . 37 A3
Shieldhill FK1 . . . . 41 B1
Wall Gdns FK1 . . . . . . 28 C3
Wall St FK1. . . . . 28 C3
Ward Ave FK2. . . . . . . 43 A4
Wardlaw Pl FK2. . . . . 15 B4
Waterfurs Dr FK2 . . . 14 C2
Waters End FK2. . . . . 15 A4
Waterside EH49. . . . . 47 A1
Water Yett EH49. . . . . 48 A1
Watling Ave FK1 . . . . 28 C3
Watling Dr FK1 . . . . . 29 A3
Watling Gdns
FK1 . . . . 29 A4
Watling St FK1. . . . . . 28 C3
Watson Pl FK4 . . . . . . 24 C2
Watson St FK2 . . . . . . 30 B3
Watt Gdns FK1 . . . . . . 29 B4
Wavell St FK3. . . . . . . 32 C3
Waverley Cres
Bonnybridge
FK4 . . . . 26 B1
Grangemouth FK3. . . . 33 A3
Waverley Pk FK2. . . . 42 C3
Waverley Rd FK5. . . . 13 B4
Waverley St FK2 . . . . 15 A2
Waverley Terr
FK5 . . . . 13 B4
Webster Ave FK2. . . . . 7 A1
Wee Row FK2. . . . . . . 30 B4
Weir St FK1. . . . . 30 C3
Wellbank FK2. . . . . . . 42 C4
Wellpark Terr
FK4 . . . . 26 A3
Well Rd FK1 . . . . 29 C1
Wellside Ct FK1. . . . . 30 A3
Wellside Pl FK1. . . . . 30 A3
Welsh Ct FK6 . . . . 10 A3
Wesley Pl FK2 . . . . . . 42 C2
West Boreland Rd
FK6 . . . . 9 C4
West Bridge St
FK1 . . . . 30 A3
Westburn Ave
FK1 . . . . 29 C2
West Carmuirs Loan
FK5 . . . . 27 C4
West Church Dr
FK3 . . . . 17 A3
Westcliffe Ct FK3 . . . 33 C4
West Dr FK5 . . . . 13 B3
Westerglen Rd
FK1 . . . . 40 B4
Western Ave FK2. . . . 30 B4
Westerton Rd
FK3 . . . . 18 B1
Westerton Terr
FK2 . . . . 7 B1
Westfield Pl FK6 . . . . 10 A3
Westfield Rdbt
FK2 . . . . 31 C4
Westfield St FK2 . . . . 31 B3
Westfield Trad Est 2
FK6 . . . . 10 A3
West Gate Rd
FK3 . . . . 18 C2
West Mains Ind Est
Falkirk FK3 . . . . 16 B1
Grangemouth FK3. . . . 16 C1
West Mains Rd
FK3 . . . . 16 B1
Westminster Pl
FK5 . . . . 6 A2
West Port EH49 . . . . . 48 A1
West Port Pl
EH49 . . . . 57 A4
WESTQUARTER 42 C4
Westquarter Ave
FK2 . . . . 42 C4
Westquarter Dovecot★
FK2 . . . . 42 B4
Westquarter Prim Sch FK2 . . . . 42 B4
Westray Terr FK1. . . . 41 A4
Westview EH49 . . . . . 47 A1
Wheatfield Rd
EH51 . . . . 38 C4
Wheatlands Ave
FK4 . . . . 26 A4
WHITECROSS 55 A4
Whitecross Ind Pk
EH49 . . . . 45 C1
Whitecross Prim Sch
EH49 . . . . 55 A4
Whitegates Pl
FK1 . . . . 28 C2
Whitesideloan
FK2 . . . . 43 C2
Whitten La EH49 . . . . 48 A1
Wholeflats Rd FK2,
FK3 . . . . 34 A2
Wholeflats Rdbt
FK3 . . . . 33 B3
Wholequarter Ave
FK2 . . . . 42 C4
Williamson Ave
FK2 . . . . 14 C3
Williamson Pl
FK2 . . . . 15 B1
Williamson St
FK1 . . . . 30 B2
Willowbrae FK2. . . . . 43 B2
Willow Dell EH51. . . . 37 A3
Willow Grange
FK2 . . . . 43 A3
Wilson Ave
Denny FK6. . . . . 9 C4
Falkirk FK1 . . . . 28 C3
Polmont FK2 . . . . 44 A4
Wilson Dr FK1 . . . . . . 28 C3
Wilson Gdns FK1. . . . 28 C4
Wilson Pl FK4. . . . . . . 26 C2
Wilson Rd FK1 . . . . . . 28 C4
Wilson's Cl 17
FK1 . . . . 30 B2
Wilson St FK3. . . . . . . 32 C4
Winchester Ave
FK6 . . . . 3 A1
Winchester Avenue Ind Est FK6 . . . . 3 B1
Winchester Ct FK6 . . . 3 B1
Winchester Dr
FK6 . . . . 10 B4
Windsor Ave FK1. . . . 29 B2
Windsor Cres
Falkirk FK1 . . . . 29 B2
Maddiston FK2 . . . . . . 53 B4
Windsor Dr
Denny FK6. . . . . 2 C1
Falkirk FK1 . . . . 29 C2
Windsor Gdns 3
FK1 . . . . 29 C2
Windsor Park Sch
FK1 . . . . 29 B2
Windsor Rd FK1. . . . . 29 B2
Wolfe Rd FK1 . . . . 31 A2
Woodburn Ave
FK2 . . . . 42 C4
Woodburn Cres
Bonnybridge
FK4 . . . . 25 C1
Redding FK2 . . . . 42 C4
Woodburn Gdns
FK2 . . . . 31 B3
Woodburn Rd
FK2 . . . . 31 A3
Woodburn St FK2 . . . 31 B3
Woodhill Ct FK3 . . . . 33 A4
WOODLANDS 30 B2
Woodlands Cres
FK1 . . . . 30 A2
Woodlands Dr
Bo'ness EH51 . . . . 37 A3
Grangemouth FK2. . . . 43 C2
Woodland Way
FK6 . . . . 9 C1
Woodlea Gdns
FK4 . . . . 25 C3
Woodside Ct FK1. . . . 30 B1
Woodside Gdns
FK2 . . . . 43 C2
Woodside Gr FK5 . . . 13 C2
Woodside Terr
FK1 . . . . 30 B1
Wood St FK3. . . . . 17 B1
Wooer St 4 FK1 . . . . 30 B2
Wotherspoon Dr
EH51 . . . . 37 A4
Wright St FK2. . . . . . . 30 B4

Y

Yardley Pl FK2 . . . . . . 14 C3
Yarrow Pl FK3 . . . . . . 33 C4
Yew Terr FK2. . . . . 42 B4
York Arc 4 FK3. . . . . 17 C3
York Dr FK2 . . . . 31 A4
York La 2 FK3. . . . . . 17 C3
York Sq 3 FK3. . . . . . 17 C3
York St FK2. . . . . 31 A4

Z

Zetland Dr
Grangemouth
FK3 . . . . 16 C2
Laurieston FK2 . . . . . . 32 A2
Zetland Pl FK2. . . . . . . 8 B1
Zetland Terr FK2 . . . . 44 A4

List of numbered locations

In some busy areas of the maps it is not always possible to show the name of every place.

Where not all names will fit, some smaller places are shown by a number. If you wish to find out the name associated with a number, use this listing.

The places in this list are also listed normally in the Index.

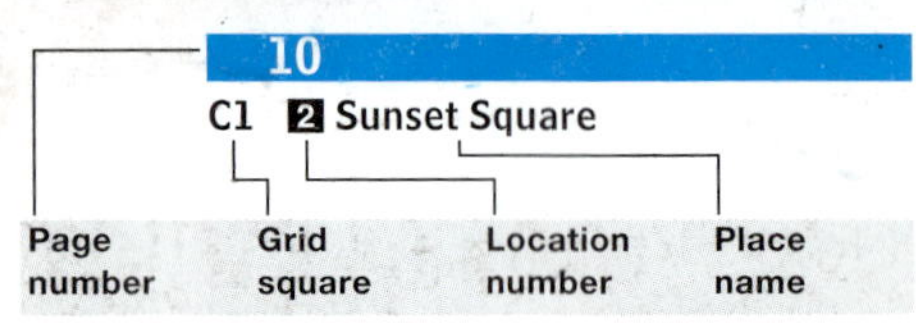

10

A3 1 Conroy Ct
2 Westfield Trad Est
3 Cruikshank's Ct

14

C2 1 Mulloch Ave
2 Anderson Ave
3 Newcarron Ct
5 Dundee Ct
6 Jarvie Pl
7 Johnston Ct
8 Gascoigne Ct

17

C3 1 Charing Cross
2 York La
3 York Sq
4 York Arc
5 La Porte Prec
7 Library La

29

C1 1 Greenhorn's Well Cres
2 Greenhorn's Well Dr
3 Greenhorn's Well Ave

C2 1 Arnothill La
2 Mayfield Mews
3 Windsor Gdns
5 Gartcows Gdns

30

B2 1 Burnfoot La
2 Kirk Wynd
3 Tolbooth St
4 Wooer St
5 Callendar Square Sh Ctr
6 Howgate Sh Ctr
7 Kings Ct
8 Mission La
9 Melrose Pl
10 St Andrews Pl
11 Pleasance Sq
12 Pleasance Ct
13 St Modans Ct
14 Comely Park Terr
15 Bluebell Cl
17 Comely Park Gdns
17 Wilson's Cl

B3 1 Silk Ho
2 Melville St
3 Melville La
4 South Melville La
5 Newmarket Ctr
6 Upper Newmarket St
7 Newmarket St

40

A4 1 Hillcrest Rd
2 Thorndene Ct
3 Seafield Ct
4 Craigburn Ct
5 Forthview Ct
6 Macpherson Pl
7 McKenzie Pl

43

A2 1 Wallace Brae Ct
2 Wallace Brae Gr
3 Wallace Brae Pl
4 Wallace Brae Gdns
5 Newlands Road Rdbt

B2 1 Bruce Gdns
2 Holmlea Ave
3 Craiglaw Terr
4 Park Gdns
5 Hillview Rd

44

A1 1 Rainhill Ct
2 Nicolton Ct
3 Ailsa Ct
4 Millbank Terr